Advance praise for
The Leader's Pocket Guide

"A sumptuous feast served up for experienced and aspiring leaders in bite-sized portions. A thoughtful and practical guide for lifting one's leadership profile in the here and now."

—DOUGLAS R. CONANT,
RETIRED PRESIDENT, CEO, AND DIRECTOR
OF CAMPBELL SOUP COMPANY AND
NEW YORK TIMES BESTSELLING AUTHOR OF *TOUCHPOINTS*

"John Baldoni gets to the heart of what it takes to inspire others to follow your lead. First you need to focus on developing yourself, building strong relationships with colleagues, and then learn to lead others, as you would expect to be led. *The Leader's Pocket Guide* is a welcome read for executives looking to lead with more smarts as well as more heart."

—RYAN M. LANCE,
CEO, CONOCOPHILLIPS

"At last—a pocket guide for leaders! With the complexity of leading in today's volatile business environment, John Baldoni's *The Leader's Pocket Guide* provides practical, easy-to-reference information for leaders to access daily. The guide covers the myriad of topics and challenges that will help leaders as they navigate the rough waters of strategy, building teams, and driving performance. It is useful and comforting for leaders of all ages and levels of experience."

—NANCY SCHLICHTING,
CEO, HENRY FORD HEALTH SYSTEM

"Executives need to take ownership of their own leadership development. John Baldoni's newest book, *The Leader's Pocket Guide*, provides a good first step. The content is rich with practical insights that are supported with action steps to provide a roadmap to implementation. A quick, easy read, *The Leader's Pocket Guide* is a handy reference for those looking to develop themselves and their abilities as leaders who can make a positive difference."

—BRIAN O. UNDERHILL,
PH.D., FOUNDER, COACHSOURCE, AND
COAUTHOR, *EXECUTIVE COACHING FOR RESULTS*

"*The Leader's Pocket Guide* is a fantastic leadership book. It is a 'must have' for all leaders. Whether you are leading a large organization, running a small business, or contemplating a new start-up, this book is full of insights that will help you avoid future pain. It is enlightening to learn from Mr. Baldoni's coaching expertise and perspective on issues we face as leaders on a daily basis. I was captivated by the 'think about' takeaways at the end of many lessons; these were like having personal executive coaching."

—JOHN OWENS,
PRESIDENT AND CEO,
COHESION CORPORATION

THE LEADER'S POCKET GUIDE

Also by John Baldoni

LEAD WITH PURPOSE:
Giving Your Organization a Reason to
Believe in Itself (2011)

THE AMA HANDBOOK OF LEADERSHIP
edited by Marshall Goldsmith, John Baldoni,
and Sarah McArthur (2010)

12 STEPS TO POWER PRESENCE:
How to Assert Your Authority to Lead (2010)

LEAD YOUR BOSS:
The Subtle Art of Managing Up (2009)

LEAD BY EXAMPLE:
50 Ways Great Leaders Inspire Results (2008)

HOW GREAT LEADERS GET GREAT RESULTS (2006)

GREAT MOTIVATION SECRETS
OF GREAT LEADERS (2005)

GREAT COMMUNICATION SECRETS
OF GREAT LEADERS (2003)

180 WAYS TO WALK THE MOTIVATION TALK
(coauthor with Eric Harvey) (2002)

PERSONAL LEADERSHIP:
Taking Control of Your Work Life (2001)

180 WAYS TO WALK THE LEADERSHIP TALK (2000)

THE
LEADER'S
POCKET GUIDE

101 INDISPENSABLE TOOLS, TIPS, AND TECHNIQUES
FOR ANY SITUATION

John Baldoni

AMACOM

American Management Association

New York • Atlanta • Brussels • Chicago • Mexico City • San Francisco
Shanghai • Tokyo • Toronto • Washington, D.C.

Bulk discounts available. For details visit:
www.amacombooks.org/go/specialsales
Or contact special sales:
Phone: 800-250-5308
Email: specialsls@amanet.org
View all the AMACOM titles at: www.amacombooks.org
American Management Association: www.amanet.org

This publication is designed to provide accurate and authoritative information in regard to the subject matter covered. It is sold with the understanding that the publisher is not engaged in rendering legal, accounting, or other professional service. If legal advice or other expert assistance is required, the services of a competent professional person should be sought.

Some content in this volume is adapted from material previously written by the author and published with CBS Interactive. This copyrighted material (Lessons 14, 23, 30, 35, 40, 42, 43, 55,56, 58, 61, 62, 76, 77, 81, and 85) is adapted with permission of CBS Interactive.

Library of Congress Cataloging-in-Publication Data

Baldoni, John.
  The leader's pocket guide : 101 indispensable tools, tips, and techniques for any situation / John Baldoni.
    p. cm.
  ISBN 978-0-8144-3231-0 (hardcover)
  1. Leadership. 2. Executive ability. I. Title.
  HD57.7.B34895 2012
  658.4'092—dc23

                          2012015320

About AMA

American Management Association (www.amanet.org) is a world leader in talent development, advancing the skills of individuals to drive business success. Our mission is to support the goals of individuals and organizations through a complete range of products and services, including classroom and virtual seminars, webcasts, webinars, podcasts, conferences, corporate and government solutions, business books, and research. AMA's approach to improving performance combines experiential learning—learning through doing—with opportunities for ongoing professional growth at every step of one's career journey.

Printing number

10 9 8 7 6 5 4 3 2 1

To the men and women I have had
the privilege of coaching.

Although my role in shaping their careers
is small, their role in shaping
my understanding of leadership is huge.

I am forever grateful.

Contents

COLLEAGUES

ORGANIZATION

Prologue

> "When we are no longer able to change a situation,
> we are challenged to change ourselves."
> —VICTOR FRANKL

FOR SOME TIME READERS HAVE BEEN ASKING ME if I would consider putting my thoughts on coaching in book form. While the idea has always intrigued me, I wanted the opportunity to do more than collect advice. I have taken the time to read and sift through well over a hundred articles and pieces I have written and distilled them into single-thought concepts that are designed to help leaders both emerging and veteran find insight, comfort, and inspiration.

The Leader's Pocket Guide reflects the issues that develop in the careers and lives of executives, and the short, to-the-point ideas followed by self-reflection mimic what I do in my leadership consulting. Interwoven into these ideas is a rich texture of practical and tactical advice.

Experienced leaders will find surprises that will stimulate them to think about issues differently and refine their leadership capabilities. New leaders will likely find this book to be fresh and lively. I hope so, but I would also remind them that those in leadership positions know far more than they give themselves credit for, and therefore this book will also provide the reassurance they are seeking.

Augmenting this book is some up-to-date research

focused on the role of leaders and the expectations that followers have for them. Recall the words of Theodor Geisel, who as Dr. Seuss wrote, "Today is your day! Your mountain is waiting. So . . . get on your way."

Enjoy the book and lead on!

SELF

"Find out who you are and do it on purpose."

—DOLLY PARTON

LEADERSHIP HAS OFTEN BEEN DEFINED as a journey. The journey begins with the starting point, and that starting point is the self.

Before you can lead others, you must learn to lead yourself. Bedrock principles of self-leadership begin with the desire to make a positive difference.

Learning what you can do as well as what you cannot do is essential to self-development. Critical to development is a profound understanding of one's abilities as well as one's liabilities. Tipping the scales on the side of ability to diminish the liabilities takes a deep sense of awareness. You hone the awareness through trial and error, or what is better known as practice.

Research Says...

According to 2011 Hay Group surveys of 4 million employees globally,

63% say:

"My job provides me the opportunity to learn new skills and develop new talents."

56% say:

"I have a good idea of the possible career paths available to me."

52% say:

"I am kept informed about what is required for me to advance at the company."

Research indicates that employees around the world have expectations for professional development. Ultimate responsibility for career development rests with the employee. It is up to him or her to take advantage of the opportunities offered.

1. | How to Know Yourself Better

LEADERS WHO SUCCEED ARE THOSE WHO KNOW THEMSELVES inside and out.

While coming to terms with yourself is a private matter, failing to come to terms with your own limitations as a leader affects your ability to lead. Here are three questions leaders can ask themselves, or a trusted associate or two, about their own managerial performance:

What more do I need? This question might seem easy because a leader will always say she needs more time. Lack of time is often an excuse for failing to address simmering issues or to carry projects through to fruition. Ask yourself and others what you need to do more of; one possible answer might be "doing less." That is, learn to delegate more and devote your time to thinking.

What else should I be doing? By focusing on less, you may learn to delegate not simply tasks, but also responsibilities. Too often executives feel they need to be engaged in the work when their job is really to engage other people. Let your people do their jobs. If they can't, find out why. You may need to find employees with different skills sets or you may need to provide your people with additional training, resources, and manpower.

How do I accept feedback? "The day soldiers stop bringing you their problems is the day you have stopped leading them," says Colin Powell. "They have either lost confidence that you can help them or concluded that you do not care."

None of us welcome bad news about ourselves and our work, but self-aware leaders are those who not only accept it, but invite it, and even seek it out. They do so because they are continually learning.[1]

Without self-learning and self-awareness
there can be no personal growth.

Think About...

How you might get more in tune with yourself.

Spend at least a few minutes every day reflecting on how the day went. What went well and what would you like to have done better?

Be mindful of feedback and make a point of thanking people who offer it.

Self-Knowledge = Insight + Practice

2. | Think More Critically

CRITICAL THINKING IS THE ABILITY TO EVALUATE OPTIONS, weigh alternatives, and make informed decisions.

Question assumptions. Critical thinkers ask questions and look to find the *what* and the *why* behind every proposition. Often we question assumptions when things go wrong. Crisis can bring out the best critical thinking because it forces you to question how and why you ended up in trouble.

Adopt different perspectives. Take advantage of the diversity represented in today's management landscape. An India-trained engineer may not view a problem the way one raised in Iowa will. Both may have the same problem-solving tool kit, but their different experiences provide valuable insights.

See potential. Busting assumptions and harnessing multiple perspectives are deductive skills. Critical thinkers should also have a creative bent that allows them to see opportunities where others see obstacles. For example, one executive may see a production snag as a problem, whereas a savvy thinker must view it as an opportunity to revamp the process to produce something new.

There is one additional aspect of critical thinking that is vital to today's leader: **managing ambiguity.** The speed of business, intertwined as it is with global factors and complex supply chains, dictates that you will never know all the variables. Therefore, you need to get comfortable with operating in an environment where change is constant and rapid decisions are required.

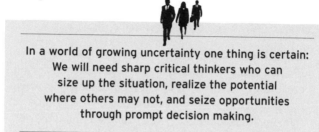

In a world of growing uncertainty one thing is certain: We will need sharp critical thinkers who can size up the situation, realize the potential where others may not, and seize opportunities through prompt decision making.

• • • • • • •

3. | Character Trumps Perfection

INTEGRITY IS THE CORNERSTONE OF SOUND LEADERSHIP. It is what gives managers the character they need to insist on doing the right thing, as well as doing it the right way.

Integrity is not a process; it is a value that is practiced by individuals, managers and employees alike. So it matters what employees do and how they do it.

As a veteran executive once told me, hire for character. Don't expect to develop something that is not there. If a person lacks a moral compass, don't think you can give him one.

Managers, like all of us, want to succeed, and because
their success is based upon getting the best people
they can to work for them, good managers are
on the lookout for talent for their teams.

● ● ● ● ● ● ●

4. Yes, It Does Matter What People Think of You

SAVVY EXECUTIVES KNOW that brand is more than a product or service; it is the sum of how and why you connect with consumers and what they think of you.

Since leaders accomplish very little by themselves, they need to bring others together for common purpose. How others perceive the leader is important to encouraging followership.

Followership, which is based upon trust, is a reciprocal act. As historian and leadership author James MacGregor Burns teaches, people follow the leader because they have similar values.

A leader's reputation, therefore, is essential to creating trust, and in turn getting people to work together to achieve mutually beneficial aims.[2]

How a leader nurtures his or her reputation
is important to creating followership.
Reputation is the sum of what a leader
accomplishes and how he or she does it.

• • • • • • •

5. | Add to Your Leadership Brand

YOUR BRAND AS A LEADER is a reflection of how others perceive you.

Leaders are judged by their accomplishments, but those achievements occur only when others believe in the leader. A successful leader's brand relies upon this reciprocity. It's important that you nurture your leadership brand in the right way. Here are some suggestions:

Communicate by example. What a leader says is important, but what a leader does is even more important. People are more likely to follow a leader who follows through on what he promises and lives with the consequences. Failure to meet a deadline isn't necessarily a failure of leadership. Failure to set the right example is.

Stand by your convictions. The true mark of a leader is what she does when things are going poorly. Acting in the name of expediency is the ruin of many a promising executive. A decision is a leadership choice. Good leaders are those who stand up for what they believe and act on those convictions. They may not always win, but you know where they stand and what they stand for.

Radiate hope and confidence. Leaders need to give people a reason to believe in themselves. Leaders are those who can look over the horizon and see the possibilities of what lies ahead. Good leaders are those who can bring others along to see it too. Viewing the future with a sense of hope and then demonstrating confidence to make good things happen is fundamental to leadership.[3]

When it comes to reputation, *how* you do sometimes matters more than *what* you do. A leader's ability to get things done right will depend upon treating people right. What a leader does is rooted in mission; how a leader does it shapes her legacy.

Think About...

How others regard you and what you do.

Leadership depends upon perception. It should reflect your inner character. But it will not unless you put your character into gear and lead by example.

Think of an example of how you showed others what it means to lead by example. What did it say about your values?

Think of three more examples of situations in which you could live your values and lead by example.

Leadership Brand = Authenticity + Connectivity

6. | Why Accountability Counts

ACCOUNTABILITY IS A CORNERSTONE of organizational cohesiveness.

A sense of accountability holds people responsible for performance and for results. Accountability lies at the root of leadership authenticity. A leader who does not hold himself accountable will find it difficult to lead others. Leadership provides a foundation for effective management: the operational rigor—processes, policies, and people—that must be in place to ensure that an organization runs smoothly.

Accountability underscores management because it reinforces getting things done right and done on time. A manager who is sloppy in his administration can try to hold people accountable for their results, but when management is loose, results will be sketchy, too.

While management is administrative, leadership is aspirational. It focuses on what must be done to ensure that the organization and its people succeed.

Accountability is essential because the leader must make difficult decisions. A leader who is not accountable to the organization will act in his own self-interest (or for a select few) rather than doing what the organization needs him to do: stand up for what is right.[4]

> Accountability matters. Not simply to the leaders but even more so to the people in the organization who look to those at the top to manage effectively and lead well.

• • • • • • •

7. | Making the Choice to Manage

MOVING INTO MANAGEMENT is a huge leap of faith.

For many employees, it means giving up what they really love doing. That's why they're considered promotable in the first place: They're good at their jobs. But too frequently managers-to-be are not asked if they really want to move up, and worse, they're not prepared to manage others. So before you consider moving into management, ask yourself three questions:

Why do you want to manage? Technically competent employees typically enjoy their jobs. Many want to continue being designers, engineers, and scientists; management to them is administrative, not something worthy of their skill set. Ask yourself if you actually want to manage, and if so, why? More money and prestige may be incentives, but they aren't enough to sustain a career.

What job will you be giving up as a manager?

As a manager you will be giving up what got you promoted in the first place. Your competence has been based upon what you do well, be it finance, research, design, or engineering. Moving into management means you will be supervising others who do what you did. You need to be comfortable with letting go of what you do well in order to help others do it.

Where will you go for support? Becoming a

manager is a big challenge. Know where you can go for help as you learn on the job. A coach or mentor could be a big assist for you. Also seek out management training programs offered through your company or at a local business school.

Those who choose to become managers eventually discover one of the hidden pleasures of management: leading a team for results. Those who succeed in this endeavor are called leaders!

8. | Making the Choice *Not* to Manage

DON'T BE AFRAID TO SAY NO!

Some employees have the gumption (as well as the self-knowledge) to say no to a promotion.

Being a manager can be one step removed from doing work you love doing. Managers spend most of their time providing resources for others to do the work. It can be rewarding, but if you would prefer to focus on your skill set then management may not be for you.

If you are comfortable in your current job and others recognize your value, you can take satisfaction in knowing that you are pursuing your chosen passion rather than becoming a manager.

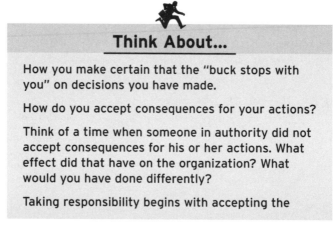

Think About...

How you make certain that the "buck stops with you" on decisions you have made.

How do you accept consequences for your actions?

Think of a time when someone in authority did not accept consequences for his or her actions. What effect did that have on the organization? What would you have done differently?

Taking responsibility begins with accepting the

responsibility to manage and lead in the first place.
Are you ready to take on that responsibility?

Accountability = Responsibility + Consequence

• • • • • • •

9. | Develop the Confidence to Lead

ACCOMPLISHMENT NURTURES CONFIDENCE.

Identifying your moments of strength is not the same as writing your curriculum vitae; graduating from college and landing a good job are highlights, of course, but when it comes to self-confidence you want to dig beneath the surface. Here are three related questions you can ask yourself to help you uncover your successful self:

What do you do well? This question opens the door for you to itemize the abilities that have enabled you to succeed to date. Focus on your talents: what you do well. For example, you may possess strong conceptual skills. You may be one who can think strategically, a person who can look at the big picture and see opportunities where others see only blue sky. Such abilities are your strengths; you owe it to yourself to recognize them.

Why should people follow you? You need a strong sense of self to lead others, so consider how you assess problems and find solutions. Look at occasions when you have mobilized yourself and your team to tackle a tough assignment. Perhaps you took on a failing project and turned it into a winner. You also may have found ways to reduce costs and improve efficiencies when others said it was impossible. In these instances, and in others you can remember, you have given people a reason to believe in your ability to get things done.

What have you done to earn the trust of others? This question should provoke a recall of what you have done to instill followership. You may have defused a conflict between two colleagues, or took the lead on a nasty assignment that no one else wanted to handle. Or maybe you went out of your way to see that senior management recognized the efforts of your team. Likely you are known as one who holds herself accountable.[5]

Consider what has enabled you to achieve what you have accomplished to date. When it comes to finding sources of accomplishment, you want to focus on the positives, your moments of triumph—those opportunities where you shone, helping yourself and your team achieve a goal.

10. | Project Confidence

Realism. Confident leaders are those who can look reality square in the face and not flinch. They possess an inner strength that enables them to size up adversity and remain true to purpose.

Reassurance. Leaders need to share their sense of confidence with their people. That does not mean that leaders must say everything is rosy. Reassurance emerges from addressing reality but also talking about what is going right and what individuals can do to improve a situation.

Resolve. The strength to persevere is a form of confidence. It does not mean that you have all the answers; in fact you may not have any, but you do know that as a leader your job is to hold the organization together until the situation brightens.

Realism, reassurance, and resolve all inspire confidence, which is something leaders should try to project every day.

11. | Three Ways to Regenerate Hope

THERE IS ONE LEADER in whom I have found nearly a boundless source of inspiration: Winston Churchill.

While history often remembers him at the height of his power as he led Britain through the terror of World War II, I like to reflect on the Churchill of 1915, tossed from the cabinet after the debacle of Dardanelles, which was an ill-fated plan to knock Turkey out of the Great War.

The Churchill of this period teaches us that we can recover from our mistakes if we take charge of our own recovery; this is something that should be familiar to any executive. However, action after adversity should be preceded by a period of reflection as well as rejuvenation. Here are three ways to make this happen:

Reflect. Take a step back, consider what happened, and examine the situation from all angles. Discuss with colleagues what went right as well as wrong. Assess your performance and consider what you might have done differently. Now that you know the outcome, use what you know to prepare for the future.

Recharge. Now, put the failure aside and find ways to reconnect with yourself. It may be through a regime of fitness or by spending more time with friends and family. Keep yourself occupied; do not dwell on yourself. Churchill painted. What might you do? Find something to reconnect your mind with your spirit. You may have lost a battle, but you did not lose your life. Keep thinking positively.

(Re)Act. You must do something. If you are in the same job, put lessons learned from failure into place. Debrief your team. If you are in a new job, find ways to leverage those bitter lessons in your new position. Know that you are a different person, in many ways a stronger one for having withstood the pressures of defeat. Channel your energies into your work, but keep in tune with yourself and the people close to you.

Understand that defeat is not the end. The Churchill of 1915 prepared the way for the Churchill of 1940 to become the savior of his nation.[6]

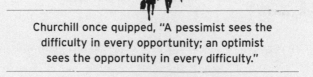

Churchill once quipped, "A pessimist sees the difficulty in every opportunity; an optimist sees the opportunity in every difficulty."

Think About...

Ways you have developed your confidence to lead.

Consider a time when your lack of confidence may have hurt you. What happened and why? What will you do differently?

Give an example of an action you took that helped you develop your self-confidence.

How do you convey your confidence to others?

Self-Confidence =
Accomplishment + Conviction

● ● ● ● ● ● ●

12. | Act Like a Leader

GOOD LEADERS HAVE A SENSE OF PRESENCE, the "right stuff" of leadership.

Presence is a combination of authority and authenticity as well as accessibility. It requires an ability to act so that others will believe you are in control.

Get out of your skin. Just as actors learn roles, leaders learn theirs. One of the first is that they need to connect to others. A manager who sits behind a desk all day issuing directions via email may be fulfilling an administrative role, but she is overlooking the personal connection that comes from conversation. Personal conversations can happen regardless of distance. Pick up the phone or take advantage of teleconferencing.

Listen actively. So much of acting is reacting to what others have to say. You will never know what people are thinking until you listen. Listening to others has seldom been as important and seldom been as neglected. But like an actor, you must focus on others so that you know what to expect from your team.

Spread optimism. People want to believe in their leaders, if only for the simple fact that it makes life easier. People want to believe that what they do matters. It falls to the leaders to provide that assurance. At the same time, if things are not going well, leaders need to be one with their teams; they need to avoid happy talk and listen.

Bottom line, leaders do what needs to be done for the good of the organization.

13. | Four Ways to Lead with Presence

LEADERS WITH EFFECTIVE PRESENCE are men and women who use their authority to bring about good things for the organization.

Here's how to accomplish that:

Know the score. Executives who talk a good game may appear to have presence, but what they really have is a silver tongue. If you seek to inspire, you need a deep knowledge of the situation.

Radiate command. A leader with presence wears authority like a well-tailored suit. Others notice the good fit and feel comfortable in her presence. A leader who cannot radiate authority is one who will struggle to create followership.

Provide hope. When people seek inspiration, they are often really seeking hope. Leaders need to deliver it to them. With hope there's a sense of possibility—that if we do what the leader asks, we will succeed.

Be humble. Exuding authority doesn't mean overlooking personal limitations. Good leaders are those who know their flaws. A sense of humility affects inspiration in one very direct way: The leader acknowledges that he will succeed only with the help of others.

A humble leader draws people to him not because he has all the answers, but because he recognizes that others have good answers, too.

Think About...

Ways you put your leadership presence into action.

Are you giving people reasons to believe in your leadership?

What have you done lately to demonstrate your faith in others?

What have you done to ensure that others believe in you?

Leadership Presence = Authenticity + "Right Stuff"

14. | Build Your Resilience

RESILIENCE IS A NECESSARY TRAIT IN LEADERSHIP, especially as businesses seek leaders who know what it means to get knocked down but have the wherewithal to get up and try again.

Here are four characteristics to consider:

Perseverance. This is the quality that will not allow you to give up, especially when there are roadblocks. Resolve is that inside drive that looks for ways around obstacles but also provides the doggedness to keep on trying.

Authenticity. People want leaders who are the "real deal." There is so much phoniness in our celebrity culture that employees become hypersensitive to those managers who play the "me-first" game: first to take credit and first to assign blame! People today look for those willing to be accountable even when bad things happen.

Perspective. There is no shame in getting knocked down. What matters is the ability to stand up again. Sometimes adversity so rattles people and so undermines their confidence that they lose perspective. There is nothing wrong with being disappointed, but when it turns into defeatism, that's a problem. Resilient leaders take the long view and never get too low when they fail or too high when they succeed. They maintain perspective.

Confidence. People develop a sense of confidence through their accomplishments. Too much confidence is hubris and turns others off. Too little confidence also turns people away because no one wants to follow someone who does not believe in himself.[7]

Resilience is an attribute that every leader needs to have; resilience is the determination to bounce back from failure and the strength to persevere.

Think About...

How you demonstrate resilience and perseverance.

Where will you find energy to persevere? How will you keep yourself motivated to pursue a difficult objective?

How long do you allow yourself to review the past and what do you do to prepare for the next challenge?

Do you engage in activities that allow you to remain resilient and roll with the punches?

Resilience = Perseverance + Practice

15. | Avoid "Coulda, Shoulda, Woulda"

IT'S OFTEN SAID that the definition of character is what you do when you think no one is looking. The same applies to grace, that sense of dignity one brings to interactions with others.

When we are disappointed, the temptation to lash out is very real. We tempt ourselves with "coulda, shoulda, woulda" when in reality those words are meaningless.

It does not matter that you lost the opportunity; what matters is what you do next. Moaning and groaning—at least for more than thirty minutes—is pointless.

Sit down and have a conversation with yourself. Consider what you did right as well as what you could have done better to earn the business. Very honestly, you may have done your very best.

So learn from the experience. Consider what you will do better the next time. And yes, that includes not applying for such work again, if you think it is outside your scope or your abilities.

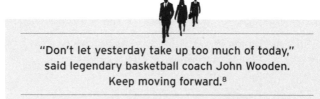

"Don't let yesterday take up too much of today," said legendary basketball coach John Wooden. Keep moving forward.[8]

16. | Get People to Believe in Themselves

GETTING OTHERS TO FOLLOW YOUR LEAD is what every leader must strive to achieve. One good way to instill followership is to encourage people to believe in themselves.

That ability was what Ronald Reagan parlayed when he ran for president. When Reagan was elected in 1980, the nation was in the grips of recession. He focused people's thinking to the future and what might be if they elected him. And he won.

Instilling the can-do spirit in others requires faith that they can do the job and a commitment to help them do it. It also requires that the leader continue to support his or her people, especially when the going gets tough. Positivism must prevail over pessimism.

People who believe in themselves and in a cause greater than themselves can achieve great things—as long as they have a well-intentioned leader to point them in the right direction.

Leaders who encourage others to believe in themselves are leaders whom others want to follow.

Think About...

Ways that you exhibit "no excuses" leadership.

Think of a specific instance in which you refused to give an excuse and instead focused on doing the job right. What did you learn about yourself?

How can you best convey that you believe in others? What actions can you take to parlay that into gaining followers? Do you engage in these activities?

What is one thing you can do to demonstrate that you have confidence in another individual?

Responsibility = Ownership + Commitment

17. | Take Charge of Your Own Fears

FEAR IS endemic to an organization facing hard times.

However, managers should not show the fears they feel to their team. It sends the wrong signal and can cause employees to lose faith. How leaders deal with fear is important.

Try these tactics to help you control your fears:

Be realistic. High achievers fear something more than business failure; they fear they will not perform up to expectations. It is critical to address that possibility. One way is to game it out in your mind. Play the "what happens if" scenario for each action step. If this happens, then what?

Or if that happens, what do I do? Rolling out the scenario in your mind may give you the comfort of knowing the consequences. So often the unknown is more fearful than the known. "Fear," goes the German proverb, "makes the wolf bigger than he is."

Confide in a friend. Talk it out with a friend, preferably not a subordinate. You can role-play the scenario with her as a means of gaining perspective. Invite your colleague to ask you questions. So often the simple act of speaking out loud is helpful. Verbalizing the situation forces an individual to frame the situation in ways that can lead to greater clarity.

Look for inspiration. Find an outlet to release your fear. Exercise is always good; keeping yourself fit is healthy. Some find hope in their faith; others find it in doing something completely different, perhaps coaching a team, volunteering at a shelter, or organizing a food drive. These things can be fulfilling because they get you outside of yourself by helping others.

Lighten up. Dwelling in fear is a zero-sum game. You must abandon that mindset. Make light of the situation. Find ways to take your mind off of it by exercising, going to a movie, visiting with friends, or simply taking a long walk.[9]

Fear is reality when dealing with tough times, but how you manage it is the measure of effective leadership. Standing up to fear, acknowledging its presence, and resolving to move forward requires determination and courage.

18. | Level with Yourself

LEADERS NEED TO BE HONEST with themselves. Understanding what you can do and cannot do is essential to leading others.

Look in the mirror. Consider what you are doing now and what you could be doing better. Do not be overly critical of your performance. Perfection is not only unattainable, it is a false ideal that leads to disappointment and grief. It is better to be realistic about what you have done and can do in the future.

Insist on candor. Hold yourself accountable for values you espouse. Invite a trusted associate or two to watch you. Ask them to check that you are "walking the talk" in matters of accountability. If you want people to trust you, consider what you are doing to earn that trust. Leadership is never easy, but when resources are scarce and financial pressures rise, it is essential that leaders be seen and heard.

Put your beliefs into action. How do you want to be remembered? Do you want to be the one who was the first to point the finger of blame, or the first to share credit with others? Do you want to be considered as one who knew the business as well as he knew his people? Do you want to be known as one who managed her career as well as she managed the needs of others?

These may be simple questions but when answered honestly they can provoke an honest dialogue. So take the time to write out how you want to be remembered, not necessarily after you pass on but when you leave your current job.

Leaders who lead from the center of their being are those who balance self-awareness with a predilection for making a positive difference.

Think About...

How you would like to be perceived by others.

Think of a specific instance in which you acknowledged your fears but maintained your composure. What did you learn from the experience?

What can you do to keep yourself focused on positive outcomes?

What is one thing you can do now to translate your personal convictions into actions in order to help others succeed?

Mirror Image = Honesty + Candor

19. | What Are You Doing to Add Value?

JUST AS COMPANIES SEEK to reengineer the value propositions of their products, managers should consider doing the same.

Companies do it by adjusting the features, benefits, and pricing of their offerings; managers do it by reevaluating the services they offer their employees. These three questions may help with the reengineering process:

How can I continue to add value to my team?
The answer comes from defining what you do now compared to what you need to do next. With more responsibilities, you need to find ways to delegate to others some of what you do. You may also need to eliminate things, e.g., reports, meetings, or travel. You need to distill your role to its essence and ration it to those who need it most. That is, you pull back from doing and spend more time advising.

What obstacles are holding me back from adding that value?
Two big obstacles typically loom: your boss and your people! You need to confer with your boss and gain agreement about your role, and especially how that may affect your relationship with her. Your people need to be preparing to make more decisions and to assume new responsibilities when you are not around.

How can I sustain that value over time?
The thinking you do to prepare and act now will be essential to the future of your team and your organization. With

less of you, everyone gets the opportunity to step up and do more decision making. For some this begins the leadership development process. For others, it could be a weeding-out process, not necessarily from the company but from future leadership. Knowing the capabilities of your team is essential.

Rethinking your value to the enterprise might be the best thing a manager can do in a recession. Return on investment is critical in times of scarcity and also lays a foundation for times of plenty.

Think About...

How you can "reengineer" the value you bring to your team.

How can you acquire new skills to improve your competencies?

What obstacles are hindering your own success and the success of your team?

What will you do differently to ensure that you keep adding value to your team?

Value = Competence + Adaptability

20. | Friends, Family, Health

THE PRESSURES OF LEADERSHIP are always there, but successful leaders find time to ground themselves. Here are three things you do not wish to neglect:

Friends. Twin concepts underscore friendship: relationship and reciprocity. We want to have relationships that are worthy of giving to and getting from. By that I don't mean we choose friends because of what they offer in terms of materialism but rather what they bring to the relationship—a story, honest talk, but most of all understanding of us and who we are as people. We reciprocate with our own unique gifts—our stories, our honesty, our understanding.

Family. You can define family as something held together by the twin ideals of love and responsibility. While poets have waxed for millennia about love, for me it comes down to simple respect. Respect for parents may come readily, but between husband and wife it is earned. Each must give something to and for the other on a daily basis. Responsibility for family, especially when children are involved, means making decisions that will benefit others before yourself. The concept of sacrifice holds families together in tough times as well as good ones.

Health. When we speak of health, it may be wise to consider three aspects: physical, mental, and spiritual. Keep yourself physically fit through exercise and a sensible diet.

Take your medicine when required. Mental fitness is essential for your productivity, and for that reason you want to exercise your mind through challenge and experience. Spiritual health is the connection to something greater than yourself, however you define it.[10]

Friends. Family. Health. It's a good framework for keeping your leadership and your life in perspective.

Think About...

What you are doing for yourself to ensure that you maintain healthy relationships with your friends and family.

Consider one thing more you should be doing with your family to ensure that you are part of their lives.

List two things you do regularly to stay connected to friends.

Holistic Leadership = Work + Others + Self

Note: "Holistic Leadership" means leadership that is focused on inclusiveness, specifically serving needs of others.

Self-Assessment

Consider the following statements and rate your level of agreement with them on a 1–5 scale with 1 being weakest and 5 being strongest.

____ I express my true character through my actions.

____ It is important to cultivate a strong sense of leadership presence.

____ I limit my priorities so that I can focus on what is important.

____ Self-improvement begins with self-awareness.

____ When I am wrong I admit my mistakes and seek to correct them.

____ I hold myself accountable for my actions even when it hurts to do so.

____ Humility is something that is necessary to create strong followership.

____ I recognize that I need to continue to develop my leadership skills every day.

____ I make time to reflect on my performance every day.

____ When you choose to lead others you must accept the consequences for what happens next.

____ **TOTAL SCORE**

+++
50   Perfect (and impossible)
49–30   Keep working
<30   Give yourself credit for being honest

Action Tips for Self

Personal development is a matter of choice. Leaders make the choice to develop their capabilities. Own the process.

- ► Find your sources of inspiration. They may come from a book or from direct observation. Keep an open mind about where the inspiration comes from.

- ► Think about how you will put your character into action to effect positive outcomes.

- ► Be realistic about your limitations. Some you can improve through education and experience. Others you will need to understand so you can work with those who have them.

- ► Be accountable for your actions, even when you make a mistake.

- ► Check your ego at the door as you hold it open for others' accomplishments to shine.

- ► Find a colleague who can serve as your trusted adviser or personal coach.

- ► Make time for reflection. Choose a regular time and place to take stock of what is going on.

COLLEAGUES

"It is no use walking anywhere to preach
unless our walking is our preaching."
—ST. FRANCIS OF ASSISI

ONE OF THE CHALLENGING ASPECTS of leadership, if not the most challenging, is leading one's peers. When you have the authority to lead, you can rely upon your position to exert authority. But when you are challenged to lead others at your own level you must rely upon the power of your purpose, that is, what you want to accomplish. Since few leaders do anything by themselves, it is necessary to build a coalition of willing partners who believe in your cause—and what's more, believe in you.

Those who are effective in leading peers are the ones who radiate competence, credibility, and confidence. In other words, they are good at what they do, others trust in those abilities, and they inspire confidence in others because they display it themselves.

Research Says...

According to 2011 Hay Group surveys of 4 million employees globally,

77% say:

"There is good cooperation and teamwork within my work group."

54% say:

"My work group receives high-quality support from other units on which we depend."

Employees around the world believe that cooperation among colleagues is important. Research shows that levels of collegiality vary. Success with colleagues then becomes a matter of personal investment—reaching out to them and finding ways to collaborate in order to achieve mutually agreed-upon goals.

21. Put Integrity and Humility into Your Ego

KEEPING YOUR EGO IN CHECK is an exercise in humility, with the emphasis on the word *exercise*.

Here are three ways to practice humility:

Accept praise, but remain skeptical. Ancient Romans had a tradition of welcoming home victorious military commanders with a state-sponsored procession that included the commander riding in his chariot. Legend has it that a slave standing next to him would hold a golden laurel above his head and whisper into his ear, "Remember you are mortal." True or not, it is a good lesson for anyone who achieves success to remind himself that success is earned, not bestowed. You need to keep earning it.

Listen to your best friend. Friends are not afraid to give each other the straight dope. Senior leaders need the friendship of one or two close associates whom they trust above others to tell them the truth. Treasure those friendships.

Reflect on your shortcomings. Take time out to gain perspective on whether what you are doing is valuable. A frank look at what you have done wrong, as it applies to decisions made, behaviors exhibited, and treatment of others, is vital to a leader keeping his head on straight. Too much dwelling on the negative is not good, but a frank assessment of shortcomings can be very helpful.

Ego affirms a leader's ability to take charge; checking the ego demonstrates a leader's ability to take charge of himself. That is critical to developing strong organizations that can achieve sustainable results.

Think About...

Ways your ego has affected how others perceive you.

Note ways your ego has helped you achieve your goals.

Consider ways your ego has gotten in the way of effective teamwork.

What can you do differently to ensure that you balance ego with teamwork?

Ego = Ambition + Humility

22. | Show Your Colleagues How to Think Critically

THE ABILITY TO EVALUATE OPTIONS is essential to effective management. Leaders can help their colleagues do it effectively by setting the right example.

Size up the situation. Knowing what is happening as well as what is not happening is essential. Senior managers who are good at their jobs do this intuitively. They drop in on a meeting, ask a few trenchant questions, solicit input, and then call for ideas.

Debate the alternatives. So far so good! Not all ideas are equal. So often successful projects are the result of genuine collaboration in which people build on each others' ideas and contributions so that the net result is a synthesis, not the product of a single mind. Debating alternatives takes time but is very necessary.

Reflect on the process. If there is one area of critical thinking that is overlooked, it is reflection. Reflection need not be saved for outcomes; it is often wise to evaluate the process as it applies to progress.

Keeping a journal helps improve critical thinking skills. The act of writing imposes two disciplines: organization and reflection. You have put down your thoughts in order and you are forced to consider your actions and their outcomes.

Teaching colleagues to think critically keeps people focused on what is necessary to get the job done right.

Think About...

Ways you employ your critical thinking skills.

Consider an opportunity to apply your critical reasoning skills to a team project.

How can you better organize your thoughts to reflect on them?

Have you challenged all of your assumptions?

Leadership Thinking = Reason + Situation

23. | Use a Checklist to Lead

SOMETIMES OUR BEST INTENTIONS get the better of us, and we end up failing to do our jobs. Often it's because we ignore the simple things.

Complexity is the enemy of simplicity, and for one good reason: it's easy to make things complicated, often because we do not take the time to think through our actions before we take them. The discipline of establishing a checklist will help you. The challenge is in using it, and that's where leadership arises.

Step by step, you can get things done if you apply your mindset.

Consider how you can improve the process by either adding things or subtracting them. Then ask yourself:

What is our goal? Always keep the outcome in front of you. When working on a project, it's easy to get sidetracked or, as the saying goes, "wrapped around your own axle." Keep the goal firmly in mind.

What can we do to simplify things? Consider what you can stop doing. It is often easier to stop doing something than to add another. By looking to remove things, you can simplify. At the same time, don't look to cut for the sake of cutting. Value comes from doing what it is right.

What can we do to ensure consistent outcomes? If what you are doing is not repeatable, you may not need a checklist. However, ensuring consistent outcomes is why we need to adhere to process. Ensuring that people know their jobs and are properly trained is essential.[1]

Good leaders do what's necessary to get things done the right way, even when it comes to following a simple set of guidelines.

• • • • • • •

24. | Use a Task List to Manage

CHECKLISTS ARE IDEAL for mapping repeatable actions, but when circumstances change you will want to be flexible.

Rather than redo the checklist, you can adopt a task list. The difference between a checklist and a task list is variability.

A checklist will stay the same from procedure to procedure; a task list will change according to circumstance.

Task-list management marries process to circumstance and in doing so provides for greater clarity between manager and employee.

Because a task list focuses on what to do right now, it is:

Intentional—how to respond to changing conditions

Actionable—what to do right now

Changeable—how to react when circumstances change.

It helps if a task list exists in written form because that will most easily provide the clarity employees need. Rewrite the task list as the situation changes, and distribute it to everyone. That ensures not only clarity but also alignment.

Managing by a task list may seem old school but in reality is cutting-edge in that it provides manager and employee with real-time updates on changing circumstances. In other words, manager and employee stay on the same page.

Think About...

The difference between a leader's checklist, which is focused on big-picture, strategic issues, and a manager's task list, which is focused on operational priorities. Both are essential to organizational effectiveness.

> What action steps would you put on your checklist to ensure that you lead more effectively?
>
> What action steps would you put on your task list to ensure that you manage more appropriately?
>
> Consider "addition by subtraction" alternatives. That is, what tasks can you eliminate in order to help the team focus on key priorities?

Leader's Checklist = Purpose + Priorities + Tasks

• • • • • • •

25. | Act Like You Own It

WANT TO MAKE A DIFFERENCE on your team?

Exert your ownership. If your boss is not giving you feedback, ask for it. If your teammates are driving you crazy, talk to them. If you are struggling with an impossible workload, find ways to lighten it. Proceeding as you are is inefficient; failing to address the problem may be even worse. Bottom line: You have a responsibility to do the job for which you are paid. Do it.

To develop a greater sense of ownership, look to yourself to see if there are things you are not doing now but could be doing that would help the team succeed. For example, do you spend more time criticizing than helping? Or do you look for excuses before helping with solutions?

Genuine ownership begins with yourself.

Nothing will ever improve unless you make a decision to act.

• • • • • • •

26. | Practice Your Troubleshooting

TOUGH TIMES ARE THE RIGHT time to practice troubleshooting. When things are not going well, it may be time to make changes. Identifying those opportunities and acting upon them gets to the heart of troubleshooting.

There are two good reasons why: first, in tough times managers are challenged to do more with less; second, managers may have more time because of the economic slowdown.

To implement your own form of troubleshooting, consider three questions:

What is the real problem? Dysfunction is often apparent. For example, a product does not perform to specification, or a process fails to deliver a consistent outcome. Diagnosing the problem requires the discipline to find the root cause. A product failure could occur because of a faulty part; a process failure could result from a missed step. You do not know until you take time to investigate.

How do we fix it? Sometimes, as with product recalls, the fix can be costly. Other times it can be solved by a simple product or process redesign. Judging what is required takes an experienced hand with strong diagnostic skills, but also savvy to understand how to achieve the most effective solution and do it expeditiously.

Who is best suited to fix it? Putting the right people on the job is essential. Not everyone is a born problem solver. You want to have people who not only like asking questions but, more important, have the facility to analyze and implement solutions. You also want people with a degree of tenacity, those who are willing to stick with it until they find a solution.

Without regular troubleshooting organizations will find themselves repeating mistakes and, what's worse, failing to capitalize on lessons learned.

27. | Stop Spinning Wheels

ONE DAY A SENIOR EXECUTIVE SHARED A BEST PRACTICE with me: turn "make work" projects into "make it work *for* you" activities. In other words, add value to the onerous.

Here's how to do it:

Itemize what you do. Do a task assessment to identify how people are really spending their time. They may be working hard, but are they doing what the team needs them to do? How much time are they spending on processes—and which processes? Sometimes we are so busy with tasks that we lose sight of the big picture.

Minimize what does not add value. We create elaborate systems that become convoluted and require so much energy to maintain that they are value detractors. Challenge employees to simplify their own jobs. Sometimes three status reports can become one. Another simple step is to reduce the number of "cc" emails you generate as well as receive.

Evaluate progress. After you have itemized and minimized, take a hard look at what you have done. Are you saving time and resources? In doing so, are you making it easier for people to do their jobs? And, ultimately, are employees contributing more value to the organization? These are tough questions that deserve thoughtful answers. Be prepared to make revisions.

Work that makes a difference is work
that others want to do.

Think About...

How you can demonstrate ownership of the
situation and its problems.

What steps can you take to ensure that your
team concentrates on what is important rather
than what distracts? How can you help team
members maintain proper focus?

What actions should you take to make work
meaningful for yourself and others?

What can you do to eliminate "make work" tasks
in order to help your team focus on "what must
be done" tasks that are critical to the success of
the mission?

Priority = Goal + Meaning + Work

28. | Act with the Big Picture in Mind

IF YOU WANT TO HAVE REAL IMPACT, you need to *act* on your ideas. Your idea, which you will translate into an initiative or a project, must contain three elements before you proceed:

First, your idea must complement the strategic direction of your company. If you work at an engineering company, your initiative should complement the engineering services your company provides. That is, do not propose buying a restaurant or opening a spa. Those might be fun to do, but they do not complement engineering.

Second, your idea must have a strong business case. What you want to do must add value to the company; that is, it must do one or more of the following: increase revenue, reduce costs, improve quality, or improve customer satisfaction. Business case rules!

Third, your idea must be blessed by your boss, or at least by someone higher up. Many bosses will welcome your initiative as long as you involve them in the process, and of course share credit with them. Also, once your boss is on board, you can lobby for the support of more senior people. That is, do not go around your boss; go *with* your boss.*

---

* Note: If your boss is a bully, do not do anything without permission. Doing otherwise could jeopardize your career.

Acting strategically will position you as a
person of influence as well as one of action.

Think About...

How you can act for the good of the team in order
to help the organization succeed.

What ideas do you have that you would like to take
to your boss?

How will you present these ideas to your boss?

$$Success = \frac{Idea + Action}{Boss's\ Support}$$

29. It Takes a Strong Leader to Compromise

COMPROMISE IS NOT FOR THE FAINT OF HEART; it takes guts to work with people with whom you disagree.

When seeking compromise, do it with an open heart. Do not let the heat of the moment, or the furor of disagreement, overshadow your attempt to bridge the divide. It is easy to get distracted by differences; it takes a keen mind to focus on areas of possible agreement. Once you find something upon which you can agree, mark the occasion as the first step toward better understanding one another.

Forging compromise requires fortitude as well as persistence, not to mention a strong stomach.

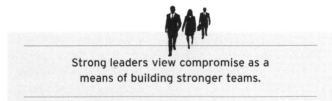

Strong leaders view compromise as a
means of building stronger teams.

30. | You Can't Say "Not My Job"!

THERE ARE THREE WORDS an executive should never utter: *not my job!*

Leaders do what the organization needs them to do. Therefore, even when they perceive that such a task—giving a presentation to a community group, visiting a low-volume customer, or participating in employee orientation—is not worthy of their executive attention, they do it. Failure to do so lets the organization down.

The "not my job" syndrome is destructive to an organization. What can you do to prevent it from surfacing and hurting morale?

Set clear expectations. Make it known that in your organization, people are expected to do their jobs as well as be open to doing things when necessary that might not fit their job description. This is especially true in smaller organizations, where bosses do many different jobs just to keep the organization running smoothly.

Be a good example. The top leader should be the first to volunteer to take on more work when the situation demands. That means the CEO may have to visit a tough customer, the head of purchasing may need to negotiate a key contract, or a marketing officer may need to pitch in with creative on a new campaign. Such assignments should not be undertaken to undermine the authority of others; they must be done when the organization needs its best and brightest to take charge.

Hold people accountable. When an executive pulls the "not my job" excuse, his or her boss must act immediately. The boss must say that such behavior is not tolerated. The organization needs people who are willing to be flexible.[2]

Saying "it's not my job" is a lame excuse. It is another way of saying, "I am too good for this." To act on such an impulse is both selfish and shortsighted. It sends the signal that you hold yourself above others. That is not only a failure of leadership, it is a lack of executive competency.

Think About...

Ways you can set the right example by accepting new challenges and remaining open to listening to others.

Consider how you can lead others to compromise by demonstrating that you are willing to assume greater levels of responsibility so the team can succeed.

Think of an opportunity when people on the team failed to compromise. What happened and why? What could you do differently?

How can you set the right example for your team by undertaking a challenge no one else wants to do?

Compromise = Team Cooperation

31. | Defend Yourself Without Being Defensive

WHEN YOU FACE CRITICISM you need to defend yourself without being defensive.

Maintaining an even keel in the face of skepticism or even hostility is a vital attribute to leadership presence, the kind of aura that you need to radiate if you ever hope to instill followership. When people are whaling on your ideas it is easy to get caught up in the heat of the moment. The challenge is not to overreact and to separate personality from ideology. Here's how:

Prepare yourself. Whenever you propose an idea there are certain to be people who do not understand the idea, do not like the idea, or simply don't like you. Prepare yourself to meet their objections. Consider who will object and why they will do it. Develop comeback arguments to address concerns. Use such arguments either preemptively (before the criticism is raised) or after the objection is voiced.

Be generous. Compliment others for the constructive feedback they are offering. You can do this even when the criticism is more critical than helpful because it shows that you are someone who is above pettiness. Others might be petty, but you are one who takes the high road. That demonstrates strength of character.

Develop patience. Few, if any, will embrace your idea as much as you have. After all, we all have our own agendas. You need to be realistic with your time frame. Know that it will take time and effort to persuade others to adopt your idea. You will hear similar counter-arguments voiced multiple times; expect it. Refine your ideas to reflect that you are listening to others.

Remember that patience also requires that you keep your cool.

• • • • • • •

32. | Practice Defending Yourself the Right Way

DEFENDING YOURSELF WITHOUT BEING DEFENSIVE will require practice.

You can do this by having a trusted colleague pepper you with questions about your ideas. This will help you refine your speaking style.

Work on relaxing your facial muscles, or even smiling—you want to radiate control.

Focus on your breathing by inhaling deeply and exhaling slowly.

Learn to speak slowly when others become agitated. Enunciate your words carefully. Savor them as you speak.

Radiate calmness when others do not.

You are not in control of how others react, but you
are in control of yourself, which is essential to
demonstrating leadership in the face of opposition.

Think About...

Ways you can argue your case without losing your
composure.

Consider times when you have lost your temper
in a business situation. How did others react?
How did you feel? What could you have done
differently?

What steps will you take before going into a
meeting where disagreements may occur to
allow yourself to remain cool and collected?

How will you make your business case so that
you demonstrate that you are in control of the
situation?

Composure > Words + Temper

33. | The Glass Is Half Full

GETTING EMPLOYEES TO LOOK ON THE BRIGHT SIDE—that is, viewing the "glass as half full rather than as half empty"—is the leader's job. Getting employees to focus on the positive is essential. Positivism is an orientation toward what you *can* do rather than what you cannot do. In leadership, positivism is more than attitude, it is initiative.

Here are three ways to instill positivism:

Never sugarcoat reality. Employees know when things are bad. If you seek to hold back information they will assume the worst. The company "grapevine" thrives on rumors, especially bad ones. Talk frankly about the business and emphasize each employee's role as a contributor. I use that last word deliberately. Address employees as contributors, not as costs.

Challenge people. Rethink the business. Invite employees to come up with ideas for improvements. Give them the authority to turn good ideas into action steps.

Look ahead. Tough times are the best time to think about who is capable of leading the organization. Such leadership is not reserved for those at the top. It will fall to the men and women who demonstrate by virtue of their ideas and their actions that they can help their companies survive, and even thrive, *now*.

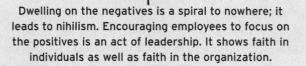

Dwelling on the negatives is a spiral to nowhere; it leads to nihilism. Encouraging employees to focus on the positives is an act of leadership. It shows faith in individuals as well as faith in the organization.

• • • • • • •

34. | How to Influence Your Colleagues

THE TOUGHEST ASPECT OF MANAGEMENT may be to persuade others to go along with you when you have no authority over them.

We as leaders in the corporate sector must do the very same. Say you are challenged to implement an initiative across multiple functions. What will you do?

1. **Do your research.** Find out what your colleagues in different functions think about the initiative. It's likely they will oppose it for any number of reasons that we can label the "don'ts." As in "Don't like it. Don't want to change. Don't want more work."

2. **Make your argument.** Demonstrate how the initiative will make things better in the long run. Acknowledge short-term pain for longer-term gain. Argue the business case.

3. **Listen, listen, listen.** Pay attention to what your colleagues are telling you. Let them digest the change but listen to how you can adjust the initiative to meet their specific requirements.

4. **Push hard.** If this initiative is important and if senior management is counting on you to drive it through, keep on it.

5. **Follow up.** This is critical. Make it known up front that you will be available to help implement the initiative. You, or your team, will help the project team get the new initiative up and running.[3]

Pushing initiatives throughout the organization is never easy, but you can do it if you are willing to listen, learn, and act on what you know.

Think About...

Things you do to instill a sense of positivism in the workplace. Positivism depends upon your actions and your point of view.

What specific actions do you take to let people know that you are willing to provide help if asked?

How can you turn around negative thoughts and attitudes in your group?

How will you show people that you appreciate their contributions?

Positivism = People + Possibilities

• • • • • • •

35. | Lead Your Peers the Right Way

DO YOU HAVE WHAT IT TAKES to lead your peers?

If you want to know how to do it right, watch how a baseball catcher works. As any baseball fan can tell you, catchers play a unique role on the team. When their team is on the field, they play a leadership role—but they are not managers. They lead by a combination of action and influence, which is exactly what you need to do in the office. So how do catchers manage this feat?

Know the strengths of others. Catchers know the pitches that pitchers can make and so, like managers, they put the pitchers in positions where they can succeed. For team leaders this means knowing what their teammates can do and what they cannot do. The leaders leverage each person's strengths so the team succeeds.

Offer perspective. By position, catchers are the only defenders who look at the game from the perspective of the batter; they can see things other fielders cannot. If peer leaders want to offer advice, they need to be able to peek over the cubicle. That is, they need to see the business as management sees it. This doesn't mean that management is always correct, but by looking at things from this perspective a peer leader can at least maintain a broader view. The peer leader then is in a position to make suggestions to teammates that are in alignment with the strategic direction of the enterprise.

Spread confidence. Make others feel good about themselves. This is especially true for peer leaders. As a peer, you know what a teammate is experiencing because often you are feeling it yourself. You know when someone needs a pick-me-up, or even a kick in the pants.

Have a sense of humor. No catcher ever made his teammates laugh more than Yogi Berra, who as a catcher won ten World Series titles with the New York Yankees. In reference to leading others as a peer, Yogi said it best: "I never blame myself when I'm not hitting. I just blame the bat and if it keeps up, I change bats. After all, if I know it isn't my fault that I'm not hitting, how can I get mad at myself?" A leader who can laugh at himself defuses tension, relaxes the team and enables people to take the work seriously but not themselves.[4]

> As a peer leader, you have earned the right to speak up as well as act for the benefit of the team.

• • • • • • •

36. | Help Your Team Avoid Burnout

THERE IS A CURE FOR BURNOUT: Shift your focus from your own success to your team's success. Here's how:

Lead, don't manage. Management is a discipline that must buttress every successful organization; things must be accomplished with people, resources, schedules, and budgets. At the same time, the top person must not be involved in all these details. He or she must lead, but empower others to manage.

Enable others. Successful people are good at what they do, which is why they have a tough time handing off tasks to others. Type A managers never let up; they revel in micro-management. Sadly, they drive good people away—and as a result, they must do more and more. But savvy leaders learn to break this cycle. Step back and let others manage not just the details, but also the decisions.

Take joy in others' success. Achieving personal success lies at the heart of ambition. But for a leader, personal success isn't really possible unless the whole team wins. When your team achieves an important goal, celebrate! Take personal satisfaction from seeing the people you have recruited and groomed succeed. Such personal satisfaction is important not only to keep your team feeling appreciated but also to enrich your own life.

There is one more thing that leaders who aspire to delegate more must do: **Drop the hero act**. This one is tough. When you do so much well, it can be tempting to think you do *everything* well. Trust me, many successful people I know truly believe they are good at everything. Acknowledging limitations may be easy for mere mortals to do, but it is hard for executives who have either built a company or risen to the top of a large organization.[5]

Accepting your limitations in any given situation can relieve stress, help you avoid burnout, and even result in better relationships with family and friends.

Think About...

Ways that demonstrate that you are a good team member.

Where could you use improvement? Why is it important that you address this concern?

Provide a specific example of how you pitched in and helped the team succeed.

What are ways you guard yourself and your team against burnout? How do you provide relief for burnout? What specific steps will you take?

How can effective teamwork contribute to a healthy outlook? What can you do to help the team keep the highs and lows in proper perspective?

Teamwork = Purpose + People

37. | Improve Team Performance

ONE THING SAVVY LEADERS LEARN EARLY in their careers is that leadership is not about self-aggrandizement. It is more about helping those around them and putting them into positions from which they can succeed.

Value them. Let people know they are important and necessary to the job at hand. Obvious, of course! But I cannot count the number of times employees have told me they have no idea what their boss thinks of their performance because he or she has never told them. Such managers are operating under the old-school rules that say telling an employee he is doing a good job is not necessary. In reality it is just the opposite; that attitude motivates good people to leave.

Push them. Give people the opportunity to excel. Doing a job is one thing; delivering superior results is another. Give employees the support they need to do the job and let them go. Note that I wrote *support*—not *resources*. The latter may not be forthcoming because of scarcity, but the former must never be withheld. Even when the employee may fail, the manager needs to provide support.

Inspire them. Good managers coach their employees; great ones inspire their direct reports. How? First, they set high standards of excellence. They push for the achievement of stretch goals. Next, they hold themselves accountable for delivering on those standards. Such leaders take pride not in their own achievements but rather in what the team accomplishes together.

Know when to claim center stage. There are times, however, when leaders—like star athletes—need to step to the fore. These are the decisions that set the direction for the enterprise. That's when a leader earns his pay grade.[6]

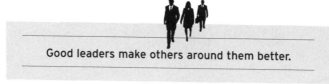

Good leaders make others around them better.

• • • • • • •

38. | Optimize Team Success

TEAM LEADERS ARE ACCOUNTABLE for team results. Here are some suggestions for improving team performance:

Honor the past. Recognize the team for what it has achieved. Make certain that individuals on the team know how much you respect them and their work. Go out of your way to make them feel welcome. Talk up their accomplishments to higher-ups. In short, make the team feel special. Compensation should reflect how well the organization regards the team's contributions.

Instill values. Critical to team success is cohesiveness, pulling together for the greater good. Make it clear that no team is above the company. At the same time, respect the fact that individual members will have greater allegiance to their own team members than to members of other teams. Managers can find ways to use that to advantage in order to stimulate higher levels of performance.

Respect the rules. High-performing teams like to do things their own way. This is a key reason for their success. Allow the team, as you would individuals, to figure out things for itself and execute its ideas in its own way. Make it clear, however, that whatever the team does must be done on time and on budget. Above all, hold the team accountable for both good and not-so good results.

Finally, **find the balance between creativity and discipline.** You want to challenge the team to think and act creatively because its ability to do new things or to do the same things with a new approach contributes to its success. At the same time, you must ensure that creativity serves the organizational purpose. The team can "freelance" methods but not objectives. Projects that it undertakes must complement the organization's mission.

Experienced managers learn the boundaries so they can keep all of their teams on a path that maintains individual team pride and benefits the entire organization.

Think About...

Ways you demonstrate that improved performance is an attainable objective for your team.

What should you do more of to help your team?

What should you do less of to help your team succeed?

How can you teach your team that collaboration is critical to team success? What example can you set so that others understand more readily?

Performance = People + Collaboration

39. | Persuade Peers—Make It Personal

THE KEY TO ACHIEVING LONG-TERM STRATEGIC GOALS is to make them present and immediate. How do you do that? You make it personal.

> **Appeal to the mind.** Good arguments begin with solid facts. If you are expecting people to change their minds—and ultimately that is what all issues of consequence involve—you'd better have your facts straight.

> **Appeal to common sense.** Make numbers real. Too often leaders who fail to persuade others to their point of view are guilty of speaking in impersonal terms (statistics) when they need to connect their ideas to individuals (one person at a time).

> **Appeal to the heart.** Facts set the foundation for rational argument, but when you are seeking to change minds you need to connect with people on a personal level.

> **Appeal to our better nature.** People like to be part of something larger than themselves, even when it involves sacrifice. This explains why people volunteer time and effort to community activities.

True and lasting change requires sacrifice. If you are going to ask people to sacrifice, you need to make certain that what you are asking is worth what they will give up.

40. | Support Your Teammates the Right Way

ALL OF US NEED A HELPING HAND, especially our teammates. Consider the following suggestions:

Listen. Sometimes all a coworker needs is your sympathetic ear. Just listening to him talk about a problem can be enough to make him feel better.

Offer perspective. Sometimes, when people make a mistake, they may feel as if their world is coming to an end—or, conversely, they may be in denial about the impact of the mistake. You can help put the issue into context, acting as the trusted friend who says, "Hey, wake up. You messed up. Make it right and move on." Caution: Just make sure you do not get caught up in a pity party or engage in a "woe is me" dialogue. Focus on how to make things better.

Give advice. Advice from a friend can be powerfully motivating, even more than it would be from a boss. You often know your team members' strengths and weaknesses better than the manager does. Focus on what you can do to help them understand their strengths as well as their areas of improvement.[7]

Advising a friend is a good thing and
when done right is a form of leadership;
that is, it helps the organization succeed.

41. Get Your Team to Play Smart Together

IS IT POSSIBLE TO HAVE TOO MANY STARS on one team?

Getting a team to work together may be more art than science. But if you have a team with lots of high achievers you need to harness their talents and ambitions for the good of the team.

Set big goals. Nothing motivates talent like a big goal. Talented people love nothing better than tackling big problems. The more difficult the obstacle, the more engaged they become. Therefore, put the goal before the team. Ask the team members how to solve it—and then challenge them to do it. Big goals are common in design, engineering, and research sectors; innovation fuels employees' drive.

Rub egos together. Smart people like being around other smart people. They especially enjoy proving how much smarter they are than the others. Use this ego to the team's advantage. Competition for scarce resources like funding and manpower will keep people on their toes.

Keep team goals first. Work to ensure that rivalries are achievement-oriented, not personal. Bruised egos are fine; hurt feelings are not. Make certain that everyone continues to feel part of the team.

Sometimes you need to **invite a star to leave**, however. Not because she is a malcontent or because she is causing trouble but because she needs to move on for the good of the organization as well as herself.

Good managers get everyone to play together well in order to achieve agreed-upon goals.

Think About...

Ways you demonstrate that you support your teammates individually and collectively.

Consider how you have helped a teammate solve a work problem. What did you do? What was his or her reaction? What did you learn?

Why is it important for individuals to commit to team goals? How can you help individuals understand the value they bring to the team?

What can you to do ensure that every teammate's ego gets to shine at least once?

People + Purpose > Problems

42. | Avoid the Niceness Disease

THERE IS A CONDITION AFFLICTING ORGANIZATIONS that often goes undiagnosed because it is perceived as benign. In truth, it is corrosive.

I call it the "disease of niceness." When I say "niceness," I don't mean politeness. Niceness in an organizational setting is the avoidance of conflict. Note that I said "avoidance," not absence.

How do you know if your company has fallen into the too-much-niceness syndrome? Here are some tip-offs:

People say, "Oh wonderful." A lot. We all like to get a pat on the back, but when affirmation is constant, you know it is nothing more than "happy talk." Utterly meaningless!

In meetings, people say, "Hmmm." That means the other person does not really like what you have to say but is reluctant to voice his doubts or opposition.

"Yeah, okay," is common feedback. We all want to hear that people like our work. But when all you get is fine, fine, fine, it means that no one is really thinking about what you have to say.

Colleagues frequently say, "No matter!" This may be the worst symptom of all—apathy. When employees cease to care, the team is in trouble. People are tuned out and are only along for the ride until they can find something better to do.[8]

Courtesy and comity are welcome in the workplace,
but do not let them serve as an excuse for
not addressing serious issues.

• • • • • • •

43. | There Is a Positive Side of Conflict

CONFLICT HAS A POSITIVE ROLE TO PLAY in every company. Very often it is referred to as "creative tension," that is, the jostling over issues that are vital to the future of the organization.

Once upon a time an executive said that if you have two direct reports who always agree with you, you do not need both of them. While not wholly true, the adage underscores the point that bosses may be served best when their subordinates feel they can debate the issues with them.

Failure to address conflicts can foster a nonconfrontational culture that is complacent. And in today's world complacency is a recipe for slow decay. Organizations thrive when its members feel they can voice their ideas even when those suggestions may be contrary to the way others think.[9]

You don't want employees throwing stones,
but you do want them to have a pebble or two
they can hurl when the status quo needs breaking.

Think About...

Situations in which conflict was healthy, and why
the conflict helped the team to succeed.

Think of a time when you wished you had received
honest feedback but did not receive it. How would
it have helped?

Consider why "straight talk" about the issues is
better than "happy talk" about nothing.

What happens when individuals are afraid to
confront issues that may harm team effectiveness? What can you do to ensure that this does
not happen?

Solution = Conflict + Collaboration

44. | Take Charge of Change

ONE REASON WE FEAR CHANGE is because we feel a loss of control. And while you cannot control the change process, you can control how you and your team react to it.

Assert your ownership. Doing so shifts the emphasis from something being done to you to something over which you have control. Consider these three questions to help you take charge:

What do we do now? Understand that you have a choice; you can opt out and not accept the change. Of course you may feel that for financial reasons (or to maintain health benefits) you cannot do this, but do understand that, unless you have been sentenced to jail, you are free to decide what to do. Making the decision to stay for whatever reason means that you have made a decision. Likewise, if you decide to leave, that is a decision.

What do we do next? Make your teammates aware of what you have decided to do. If you are staying in, you want to make certain your boss knows that you are still part of the team. If your disappointment is evident, as it might be with a loss of a promotion, acknowledge it but do not dwell on the negativity. Reassure the boss that you are still in the game and want to be considered as a contributor. Such behavior will mark you as one who has a strong sense of self and can deal with disappointment.

How can we make this work for us? Consider
how you can turn the situation to your advantage. Look
for ways to turn the change into new opportunities.
Find ways to assert your can-do spirit. Be proactive.
Look for ways to make a positive difference.

Owning the change process and making it work
for you is critical to demonstrating resilience
as well as an ability to move forward. It is
very definitely a mark of leadership.

Think About...

Times when you have felt rolled over by change
because you failed to realize it was coming.

What did you learn from the experience? What
could you have done differently?

Can you find ways to assert ownership over change
to benefit yourself and your team? Why is this
important?

Self + Control ≥ Change

45. | It Takes a Good Problem Solver to Compromise

WHEN THE PROBLEMS ARE SIGNIFICANT, recall what Henry Ford once said. "Don't find fault, find a remedy; anybody can complain."

Leaders can adopt a three-question approach to problem solving:

- What are the issues that divide us?
- What are the issues that unite us?
- What can each of us do to find solutions that improve the lives of those we lead?

Common purpose calls for common sense, but there cannot be any sense if people are not willing to listen without prejudice to what others have to say.

When people of different opinions and ideas come together to solve problems rather than create more, they demonstrate that they value constructive dialogue over divisive partisanship. Better yet, they demonstrate that they are willing to put aside differences in order to find solutions that benefit others, perhaps more than themselves.

Common purpose calls for common actions as well as everyone pulling together in the same direction.

46. | Three Ways Strong Leaders Put the Team First

COMPROMISE IS ESSENTIAL to the negotiation process. Here are some ways to implement it:

Think "outcome." When parties enter into negotiation they seek the best for their side. This is natural but it overlooks the needs of the other side. When negotiations become stalled it is prudent to consider alternate viewpoints. A good way to do this is to consider what both sides want.

Find common ground. Knowing the outcome gives negotiators a starting point for what they wish to achieve. From there it becomes a process of negotiation, generally moving toward the middle. This may involve both sides giving up something to get something in return. Shared sacrifice is important; there has to be some "shared pain" so that both sides have a vested stake not only in the outcome but also in the process.

Celebrate the union. Too many negotiations can end up as "winner take all" games, that is, the winner gets everything. That may work for one-time transactions, like buying or selling a car, but it is not sustainable within an organization. You want to leave the other side with something, if only a sense of respect.

Compromise, on the whole, is a positive. And although

we have dissected it as a process, there is more art to it than science. The art comes from creative thinking about ways to persuade the other side. It also comes from seeking to read the intentions of adversaries and turn them into allies.

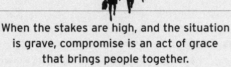

When the stakes are high, and the situation is grave, compromise is an act of grace that brings people together.

Think About...

Situations in which you have been the one to initiate compromise.

What role does compromise play in your organization now?

What did you learn from working with others to compromise? What did you learn when you failed to compromise?

What examples can you find in your own life in which compromise led to successful outcomes?

What can you do to teach others the value of compromise?

Compromise = Win + Sacrifice

47. | Help Colleagues Gain Outside Perspective

SO HOW CAN A LEADER ADOPT A DIFFERENT VIEWPOINT? How can she look at familiar things—resources, employees, structures, and even roadblocks—with fresh eyes? Let me offer some suggestions.

Know your limitations. Understanding that there are different viewpoints on issues is step one in realizing the need for new perspectives. It has been said that what keeps senior leaders awake at night is not what they know, but rather what they do not know. Knowing the limits of your own knowledge is important.

Make customer visits. Spending time with customers is an obvious way to see the world with new eyes, but so often those at the top think it is not their job. If you want to know what customers think of your work, ask them. That will take having a few conversations as well as spending time getting to know them and their needs.

Invite outsiders in. For your next departmental meeting, think about ways you can introduce your folks to outside thinking. Having industry experts speak about trends in your industry is a good first step. But think further afield. For example, the healthcare industry has studied hotel and food companies for lessons in hospitality and food preparation.

These steps can help leaders adopt a new perspective, but

they will not negate the fact that the leader is responsible for initiating change. Thinking like an outsider has its merits, but acting like one does not.

> Leaders take ownership of the issues and make the changes that are necessary.

• • • • • • • •

48. | Turn Small Talk into Smart Talk

ONE OF THE THINGS YOU CAN DO TO POSITION YOURSELF and your teammates for success is to learn how to make small talk with senior executives. Preparation is essential.

Do your homework. Learn the issues the senior team is focused on. Ideally everyone in the company should know the strategic priorities. Bone up on these so you know them, too. Think in advance about what you will say to a senior team member if you meet her in person.

Work out a key message about your projects, your career, and yourself. This is good practice whether or not you meet a senior executive. If you expect to be in a more social meeting, you might try to learn of a boss's personal interests—hobbies, sports she likes, or volunteer activities.

Be yourself. When you are introduced to the senior leader, make eye contact as you shake hands. Smile and act relaxed. Feel free to ask questions about what's going on in the company. If appropriate, talk about what you are working on. This is your opportunity to use your messages. Strive to be brief and to the point.

Read the situation. Keep speaking if the boss is interested; if not, thank the person for his time and move on, even if you didn't get the opportunity to use your key messages. In some ways your sense of decorum is more important than what you say. Rattling on when no one is interested marks you as lacking in self-awareness; knowing when to end the conversation says much about your ability to read the situation.

The good news is that what works for prepared encounters also works for impromptu ones. Just assume that someday soon you will run into a senior person, and prepare for it as you would for a more predictable encounter. That preparation will pay off in other contexts too, such as during team meetings or conversations with clients.

That's why you should **practice your key messages from time to time**, maybe on your drive to work. You can even practice by recording them on your mobile phone, just to find out how you sound. The exercise will give you confidence that you have what it takes to have a clear and coherent conversation with people in power.[10]

Success depends upon those who can
not only think creatively, but also have the skills
to put their ideas into action.

Think About...

How you connect with your colleagues in ways that
affirm their value to you.

Give an example of a time when you were able to
provide a perspective on an issue that others may
not have considered. What happened? What did
you learn from the experience?

Give an example of a situation in which you
made small talk with your bosses that helped
you connect more authentically.

Consider developing a few talking points about
what you do for the organization that you can use
next time you meet a senior executive.

$$\text{Perspective} = \frac{\text{Me} + \text{You}}{\text{Reality}}$$

49. | Lead Through Your Boss

CAN YOU LEAD if you don't have a title?

Leadership rising from the lower ranks is a hallmark of military history. Battles have been won when those under the command of others rose up and took charge. Such are the lessons of military history, but translating them to the corporate or nonprofit workplace is not so easy.

You can do this by working through your boss. You keep her in the loop about what you are doing and why you are doing it. Your ideas must complement the strategic direction of your company. That is, you push initiatives that help customers, employees, and stakeholders. You lead first and foremost with your ideas, backed by your gumption.[11]

Leading from the middle is not an easy proposition, but savvy managers can make it easier by making it safe for others to lead. Employees then can take up the challenge if and when they feel they must act for the benefit of the organization.

50. | How to Sell an Idea to Your Boss

ONCE YOU HAVE ESTABLISHED YOURSELF as a credible performer, there are three things you can do to give your big idea a better chance of success:

Align with corporate objectives. Whatever you propose for your company must complement its strategic direction. Build the business case for your idea by showing how your idea does not conflict with current priorities, but in fact supports them by planning for the future.

Work through your boss. Once your business case is well along in development, you are ready to pitch it up through the organization. But do not go around your boss, tempting as that might be in some cases; go through him. Walk the boss through your plan and get his feedback. Incorporate his ideas if they are viable. Find ways to make sure your boss gets some credit for the idea, too. These steps will help you win his backing.

Build coalitions. Things get done in organizations because people pull together to get the work done. The same goes for driving initiatives. Enlist the support of peers to help you get your idea off the ground. Leverage your customers; these are the people who will benefit from your idea. Frame your idea around serving their needs more comprehensively.

Management and employees work best when they both understand that good ideas can come from anywhere in the organization, and that those companies that capitalize on them are those that will succeed.

Think About...

Actions you have taken to demonstrate to your bosses that you are a big-picture thinker.

Consider examples of situations in which you have seen people lead without a title. What was the reaction of others?

Give an example of a time when you persuaded your boss (or your boss's boss) to support one of your ideas or initiatives.

What project do you have in mind that you would like to pitch to your boss? How will you broach the topic? What will be your business case?

Leading Up = Thinking Like a Boss

51. | How to Recognize the Signs of Hubris

CONFIDENCE IS AN ATTRIBUTE that every leader needs to embrace and to foster in others. But when confidence goes too far, it can become hubris.

Many leaders veer into hubristic behavior without realizing their shortcomings. We may be well intentioned, but we all suffer from blind spots. So how can leaders know when their own confidence is verging on hubris? Here are some warning signs:

You make many decisions independently. No, dithering isn't good. But bosses who make all of their own decisions without speaking to others are asking for trouble. How much do you ask for others' input?

You can't remember the last time you spoke to a customer. Failure to discover what people think about what you offer is not only foolhardy, it's a recipe for failure in the future. If you think you're "too busy" to connect with customers, that's a warning sign.

You always have lunch with the same people. Socializing only with select peers cuts you off from people who might offer alternate views.

Your team always seems to agree with you. If no one has contradicted you in a while, you may have inadvertently created a no-bad-news culture. Surrounding yourself with people who can do only one thing—nod—is an invitation to disaster.

When something goes wrong, the first thing you ask is, "Who's responsible?" This may be a sign that you overemphasize accountability at the expense of problem solving—which your team may see as finger-pointing.[12]

Leaders must believe in themselves, but too much belief in one's abilities can be harmful.

52. | How to Cure Yourself of Hubris

NOTHING TURNS OFF YOUR COLLEAGUES FASTER than your own sense of self-importance.

So what can you do?

Start by asking people to talk back. Employees need to be able to tell their bosses what they really think. Bosses who make people uncomfortable about telling the truth are asking for trouble. They end up sandbagging reality. So take it a step further—insist on straight talk. Candor can be cleansing in that it clears out the haze of "smoke and mirrors" that organizations tend to create.

Make time to walk the halls, talk to customers, and speak with vendors.

Get the straight dope on how the company is performing. Do not take internal reports at face value. Sometimes reports are created to shield the guilty from accountability. Use your own "walk the beat" approach to find out the truth.

Finally, remember that once your stakeholders start talking more openly, it's your job to listen. That action affirms your interest as well as your faith in others.[13]

Too much confidence is a toxic cocktail, one that can lead to the very long hangover we call hubris.

Think About...

Ways you can avoid taking yourself too seriously and why that will be important when it comes to leading others.

Think about a time when you let your ego get in the way of making the right decision. What happened? What would you do differently now?

What is one thing you can do to avoid appearing to be arrogant?

What behaviors can you show to demonstrate that you are approachable and welcome alternative points of view?

Hubris = Ego − Humility

53. | Coach Your Colleagues

PEER COACHING is a process by which one colleague serves as a trusted adviser for another. Peer coaching requires mutual trust and is nurtured by patience and practice.*

Peer coaching involves three key principles:

1. The advice given is straightforward and candid.

2. Peer coaches offer advice that benefits the organization; that is, they advise doing what is best for the team rather than the individual.

3. Peer coaches have one another's best interests at heart. Therefore they can be honest as well as supportive.[14]

Peer coaching enables colleagues to learn more about their strengths as well as their opportunities for improvement.

---

* Peer coaches may advise one another or they may choose other coaching partners.

Think About...

How to put peer coaching into practice.

- **Observe**—watch what your colleague is doing

- **Dialogue**—discuss what you observe

- **Question**—ask questions

- **Suggest**—offer your ideas for improvement

- **Challenge**—challenge your colleague to develop her own solutions and methods

Coaching = Investment in Others

Self-Assessment

Consider the following statements and rate your level of agreement with them on a 1–5 scale with 1 being weakest and 5 being strongest.

_____ My colleagues want to work with me.

_____ My colleagues say that I know how to collaborate with others even when it means putting aside my own ideas.

_____ My colleagues look to me for clear directions.

_____ My colleagues would say that I help them do their jobs better.

_____ My colleagues say I look to lead my boss and my peers.

_____ My colleagues believe in my expertise and trust me to be correct on the technical issues.

_____ My colleagues view me as someone who knows how to bring out the best in others.

_____ My colleagues regard me as a go-to person to get things done right.

_____ My colleagues say that I am one who puts the interest of the team before my own interests.

_____ My colleagues know where I stand on the issues and while they may not always agree with me, they respect my position.

_____ **TOTAL SCORE**

+++

50	Perfect (and impossible)
49–30	Keep working
<30	Give yourself credit for being honest

Action Tips for Colleagues

Leading peers can seem at times like herding cats. It may not be easy but it is necessary. Work on it!

- Communicate your intentions and confirm them with your actions. In other words, do what you say you will do.

- Listen to what others are saying, not what you think they are saying. Be careful to listen to the whole story before you draw conclusions.

- Ask questions to elicit information and create avenues of inquiry. (Drop the prosecuting attorney act.)

- Defend your positions but be willing to act for the greater good. Compromise is healthy for the team.

- Lead by including others in your decision making and your action steps.

- Be the go-to person for your team.

- Look for opportunities to make a positive difference.

- Focus on getting the work done rather than who gets credit for it.

- Show no tolerance for the blame game. It is the surest way to make enemies.

- Make your presence felt; that is, let people know that you are available to pitch in and help the team.

ORGANIZATION

> "No institution can possibly survive if it needs geniuses or supermen to manage it. It must be organized in such a way as to be able to get along under a leadership composed of average human beings."
> —PETER DRUCKER

WHAT DOES IT TAKE TO LEAD an organization? A commitment to service, specifically a willingness to put the organization first so that it succeeds.

In good times this is a straightforward proposition; it is less challenging to be in charge when the wind is at your back. In fact organizations in such times can be said to lead themselves.

But when the winds shift and times become tough it takes a leader who can provide the guidance that others need. Such leaders are purposeful and driven. They know the mission and are committed to fulfilling it.

Such leaders are ones who work through others, not over them. They bring people along giving them the resources they need to manage and succeed. Such leaders spend time coaching their people, directly when they work one-on-one with employees and indirectly when they create conditions for the entire organization to succeed.

What does it take to lead an organization? The commitment to making the positive difference for oneself, the team, and the organization.

Research Says...

According to 2011 Hay Group surveys of 4 million employees globally,

74% say:

"My immediate supervisor's behavior is consistent with our company's values."

72% say:

"I have trust and confidence in my immediate supervisor."

62% say:

"I have trust and confidence in this company's senior management team."

60% say:

"Day-to-day actions of management where I work are consistent with their words (e.g., they 'walk the talk')."

Employees around the world hold their leaders to high standards. And as this research indicates, behaviors of senior leaders do not match behaviors of employees' own managers. Delivering the level of leadership that employees demand is a leader's responsibility.

54. | How to Instill Purpose in Your People

PURPOSE IS THE FOUNDATION LEADERS use to create vision, execute the mission, and cultivate values that hold people accountable.

Purpose is what shapes the culture—its beliefs and organizational norms. That foundation is essential, because it opens the door for an organization to focus on what it needs to do to succeed.

Leaders instill purpose by communicating it through their behaviors When employees see their leaders doing for others—especially when it comes to the heavy lifting—any excuse they may have for not participating is negated.

Organizations need employees who are engaged; that is, they come to work with a sense of purpose that comes from knowing that what they do matters to others. When employees are engaged in their work, they enjoy what they do and are more productive.

Purpose is not something that should be allowed to sit on a shelf to be admired. Rather, it should be a catalyst for stimulating creativity, engagement, and strategy in ways that drive results.

55. | Make Your Leadership Relevant

PURPOSEFUL LEADERSHIP DEPENDS UPON RELEVANCY and connection. Leaders can consider three factors: context, circumstance, and consequence.

Leaders need to be flexible and apply a leadership style that fits the situation, as posited by author and organizational theorist Paul Hersey.[1] Here are some guidelines:

Context determines plan of action. Executives need to know the backstory, that is, what happened before they arrived on the scene. Sometimes it requires digging and asking lots of questions. For leaders of long tenure, knowing the context is second nature. They live it every day. Knowledge of the situation and its context sets the stage for what the leader does next.

Circumstance—the current situation—determines your degree of involvement. Crisis calls for bold actions. For example, if a new marketing program fails to generate sufficient awareness, the chief marketing officer should handle the situation. If multiple marketing initiatives fail, the CEO needs to find a solution quickly. He or she should take charge and find a new senior marketing executive.

Consequence is what happens when a leader acts. With apologies to Sir Isaac Newton, not every leadership action has an equal and opposite reaction. Very often a CEO decision is designed to turn the enterprise around or keep it on course; a frontline manager's decisions are the equivalent of trimming the sails. A CEO who makes too many decisions not only creates lots of activity, specifically churn, he also undermines the authority of other senior leaders.[2]

Considering context, circumstance, and consequence is a good way for a leader to determine how involved to be and what style to employ.

Think About...

The ways purpose provides focus, direction, and goals to employees and teams.

Have you ever been a member of a purpose-driven team? How did it feel? Can such an experience be replicated? If so, how?

What one thing can you do personally to instill purpose in others?

How can you use your next off-site to think about ways you can engage the power of purpose to help your organization focus on achieving intended results?

$$\text{Purpose} = \frac{\text{Vision} + \text{Mission}}{\text{Values}}$$

56. Connect Authentically

THE ONE-TO-ONE AUTHENTIC CONNECTION is essential to creating genuine followership, and it behooves leaders at every level to cultivate it one colleague at a time.

Be the first to break the ice. Too often I have seen CEOs stride through a row of cubicles or a shop floor without looking from side to side, and if they make eye contact with some employee, they stare back without a hint of a smile. That sends a strong signal to an employee that "you don't matter." Rather, find ways to converse. Get ready to speak up.

Keep it light. The conversation opens with a light note, something about the weather or the work they do. Smile as you speak. Once you have built a sense of rapport, you can continue the conversation. And here is where exceptional leaders truly shine; they can make the person they are speaking to seem like the most important person in the world. That builds the self-esteem of the employee and affirms his or her faith in the leader.

Ask the power question: How can I help you do your job better? This question signals that the leader understands that success depends upon both the individual and collective contributions of all employees. Employees may need more in the way of resources and less in the way of bureaucracy. It is up to the leader to pay attention. You are not obligated to do everything an employee asks, but you are obliged to listen.

Listen more than you speak. Once a leader has opened a line of dialogue, it is important to drop rank. Listen to what the person is saying. So often it is said that what CEOs fear most is not what they know, but what they *don't* know.

Speaking to frontline employees is a great way to find out what customers are saying, how products are performing, and how corporate initiatives are faring. That requires an ability to clam up and listen.

57. | How to Ask Good Questions

EVERY LEADER I KNOW has at least one need in common with other leaders: a need to connect honestly with others.

A way to foster good connections is to ask good questions. Leaders who excel at asking good questions have honed an ability to cut to the heart of the matter in a way that disarms the person being interviewed and opens the door for genuine conversation.

Be curious. Executives who do all the talking are those who are deaf to the needs of others. Sadly, some managers feel that being the first and last person to speak is a sign of strength. Just the opposite is true. This behavior cuts off information at its source, from the very people—employees, customers, vendors—who have the most to say. Your curiosity encourages them to speak up.
Be open-ended. Leaders should ask questions that get people to reveal not simply what happened, but also what they were thinking. Open-ended questions prevent you from making judgments based on assumptions, and can elicit honest answers. Using *what*, *how*, and *why* questions encourages dialogue.

Be engaged. When you ask questions, act like you care. Yes, *act*—show that you are interested with affirmative facial expressions and engaged body language. This sets up further conversation and gets the individual to reveal information that could be important.

Dig deeper. So often executives make the mistake of assuming all is well if they are not hearing bad news. Big mistake. It may mean employees are afraid to offer up anything but good news, even if it means stonewalling. So when surprising news surfaces in your dialogue, dig for details. But avoid recrimination. You are there to learn, not prosecute. Get the whole story.

Remember, problems on your team are,
first and foremost, your problems.

Think About...

Ways you can demonstrate authenticity in the workplace.

Give an example of how your authenticity enabled you to connect more effectively with your team.

What questions can you ask to make it safe for people to speak about their challenges at work?

Consider behaviors you can employ to demonstrate that you are the right leader for your organization.

Authenticity = Authority + Accessibility

58. | Manage with the Door Open

EXPERIENCED LEADERS LEARN TO CREATE an open-door policy that really means open.

Openness demonstrates three things to employees: one, you are engaged in the leadership; two, you are open to new ideas; and three, employees have a voice.

Visit people where they work. Nothing conveys importance to an employee more than senior leaders showing up on their floor or in their conference room. It conveys that the employees are important to the organization. It also helps reinforce collegiality and contributes to more open communications because the environment is familiar to the employee, not stuffy and formal like a corporate boardroom.

Invite folks to your office. Bringing an employee into the corner office connotes that you value input from others and that you value the input of this individual, so much so that you brought him or her into your office. That is an esteem-building exercise for any employee.

Play host. I'll never forget working with a business unit president responsible for some $2 billion in revenues, who upon meeting me for the first time asked, "Can I get you a cup of coffee?" He, not his administrative assistant, was getting one for himself and everyone else in the meeting. Instantly, I felt part of the team.[3]

Leaders who make a habit of walking the halls
literally and figuratively are leaders who are in
tune with what is happening and much less likely
to be blindsided by the unexpected.

● ● ● ● ● ● ●

59. | Visit Employees Where They Work

WHEN A SENIOR EXECUTIVE VISITS a subordinate in his or her place of work it sends a strong message. It demonstrates that the leader values the subordinate as a person. Here are some suggestions to help you decide when and why to visit a subordinate.

To clear the air. People who work together have disagreements. While it often falls to subordinates to try to smooth things over, when the boss makes the first move and goes to the employee to do it, it conveys a sense of "we're all in this together."

To ensure clarity. Some issues require face-to-face interaction as a means of checking for understanding. The boss's actual presence may encourage good dialogue that allows each party to ask questions. Many leaders also look for nonverbal cues such as facial expressions and body language that indicate how the listener is receiving the information, either favorably or unfavorably.

To deliver bad news. No one ever likes to give bad news, so when a boss makes a point of going to the employee directly on his turf to give him unpleasant news about a project cancellation, a budget cut, or a headcount reduction, it communicates that he cares about the people on his team.

To celebrate. Visits from the boss need not be reserved for tough times; good times are occasions for celebration. When a boss visits the team members at their workplace to congratulate them for a job well done, it's a good thing. Employees remember it.

Visiting with employees in their work space is a good habit that not only shows respect but also allows the leader the opportunity to get an up-close and personal look at how the work is going. If a leader is dispensing praise, or even advice, it demonstrates to others that the boss is one who values people as people. The personal touch is essential in establishing rapport and building trust.

Think About...

How you can connect more authentically with your people one-on-one.

In what ways can you make it safe for direct reports to bring work-related problems to you?

What can you do to make time to visit people where they work?

How can you make time for people to visit your office?

$$\text{Connection} = \frac{\text{You} + \text{Employee}}{\text{Location}}$$

60. | Lead for Engagement

ENGAGEMENT IS CRITICAL TO THE SUCCESS of your enterprise. Encouraging is a leader's responsibility.

Explain the big picture. Senior leaders are privy to what their company does and how its actions impact the lives of stakeholders—customers, employees, and shareholders. Most other employees do not know this information unless they take the time to read all of the company's communications collateral. And even then it is vague. Management must talk up what the company does and how it affects people's lives.

Communicate. Keep employees in the loop about what is going on. Take time to discuss what is going right as well as what needs to improve. Invite employees to contribute suggestions for improvement. Create loops of feedback so people can see how their suggestions are implemented. Management is under no obligation to implement every suggestion from every employee, but keeping people apprised of the status of their suggestions is critical.

Celebrate. When you achieve a milestone, mark it. This is especially important during long and difficult initiatives, particularly those involving new products and services or even organizational transformation. By establishing milestones and recognizing them, you give people a sense of progress.

Engaging the workforce opens the door
to leading more effectively.

• • • • • • •

61. | Make Your Off-Site More Engaging

AN OFF-SITE MEETING IS A GREAT WAY to instill purpose and drive engagement in your organization. To make it a success, you should consider doing the following:

Determine your agenda. Assess where you and your company stand, and what issues you want to focus on during the retreat. Just as it is necessary to consider what you want to accomplish, it is important for you to examine the future of the organization. Does the company vision still resonate? Is the mission still applicable? What opportunities are you overlooking?

Include top executives. Retreats need not be solo efforts; a close-knit team can make the time even more productive.

Invite outsiders. Sometimes it is effective to bring in guests to speak to your senior team. These folks may specialize in issues facing the organization, such as leadership or strategy. They might be from academia or the world of the arts. The expertise the outsider brings is seasoning for the stew. It encourages people to think about something other than the business at hand as a means of gaining perspective on the current situation.

Encourage honest debate during the retreat. Develop a forum during which the issues can be discussed openly and honestly. Assign executives questions and invite them to work with a colleague or two to develop specific solutions. Then present the solutions to the entire group and ask for feedback. Respect the rights of those who propose as well as those who disagree.

Follow up. After the retreat, write down what you learned. Everyone who participated in the session can be asked to do the same. Share reflections. Such ideas may lay the foundation for new ways of thinking that can influence how the company approaches problems.

Off-sites can help employees understand the purpose of their organization and their role in it.

Think About...

Ways you can improve the level of employee engagement in your workplace.

Consider specific actions you should take to improve engagement in your own team.

What steps can you take to make your next off-site more meaningful for attendees? Consider activities that bring people together to solve common problems.

Identify senior leaders you wish to come to your next off-site. What will you have them speak about, and how will you ensure that they have time to listen to what your people have to say?

Engagement = Purpose + Commitment

62. | Avoid Micromanaging Anything

ARE YOU A MICROMANAGER or just attentive to details? How can you get involved without being seen as a micromanager?

Determining how involved to be in the day-to-day details without undermining your direct reports can be a tricky proposition. Consider these guidelines:

Focus on your expertise. Part of knowing your expertise means knowing your limitations. In such instances, it is better to defer to "the experts on the ground," that is, those responsible for doing the work—designers, engineers, financial analysts, and the like.

Keep your hand in it. One senior leader I worked with struggled for a time with letting go of his pet projects. He is a gifted manager and had no problem delegating, save for one area: negotiation. He was a talented negotiator and had made a name for himself. His compromise was to delegate all but the biggest negotiations, saving some of the detail work for himself where his intervention was appropriate.

Find your source of energy inside. Feeling a sense of accomplishment as a senior leader is a matter of mobilizing the team to action and achieving intended results. This can become a slog, especially when projects hit roadblocks or resources become scarce. Also, people issues can complicate productivity. This is where the leader rises to the fore.

By focusing the team and its management on results,
the leader applies attention appropriately.

Think About...

Ways you can delegate authority and responsibility
to others.

Consider a specific action you can take to become
a more effective delegator. What responsibilities
will you delegate and why will you do it?

What tasks do you think you can help your team do
more effectively? How much time should you
spend on such tasks?

How will keep yourself motivated in order to keep
your team focused on the right issues at the right
time?

Delegation = Authority + Responsibility

63. | Don't Let Conflict Ruin Your Team

TO A DEGREE DISAGREEMENT IS A GOOD THING; it is an indication of a healthy relationship when a boss is open to alternative points of view, and the employee can offer them without fear of reprisal.

But when the situation deteriorates to the point that a boss and employee are not speaking or their friction threatens office harmony, then it is time to act.

The first step is to diagnose the situation. Conflicts over issues may be healthy, but conflicts over personality and work style are not. These call for the right person to intervene. The boss's supervisor must act to discover why the boss and direct report are in disagreement.

The second step is to use a conflict resolution model that works. The one I describe here was recommended to me by Val Markos, an executive coach based in Atlanta. If the two parties are willing to work on a resolution, ask these three questions:

- *Which of your behaviors is damaging the relationship?*

- *Which of the other's behaviors is damaging the relationship?*

- *Would you be willing to stop doing one of your damaging behaviors if the other is willing to do the same?*

The outcome of such an intervention does not rest on words. The two parties must commit to resolution and prove it through their actions. It may take time to show results, but small steps toward agreement can make a positive difference.

If no resolution is forthcoming, it will be up to the supervisor in charge—the boss's boss—to take immediate action. If the manager is not doing his part, then the boss's boss must remove him from a position of authority. If the employee is not working toward an agreement, the supervisor can allow the manager to remove the employee from his team.[4]

Conflicts between employees are not easy to resolve, but they must be. The good of the team should not have to suffer because of the conflicts of its members.

64. | Questions for Leaders Facing Long Odds

LEADERSHIP IS NOT A POPULARITY CONTEST. The mark of a good leader is how he leads against the odds or even against popular convention.

As much as we admire leaders for exerting leadership against the odds, there are times when a leader who goes against the grain may face disappointment. To avoid it, ask three key critical questions that will assert your right to lead.

What am I doing? Leaders need to support the mission of the organization, so their strategic direction needs to support what the organization is in business to do. If it does not, the alternative is to change the mission. Lou Gerstner did that as CEO of IBM when he shifted the company's focus from selling hardware and software to providing integrated IT solutions and services.

Why am I doing it? Yes, put the organization first! Leaders have personal agendas, but those agendas need to support the aims of the organization. If they do not, a leader may get too far out ahead or be seen as a lone wolf. More specifically, people are not eager to support someone who they perceive is working only for herself. That makes the process of getting rid of the lone wolf all the more pleasurable.

Is it worth it? This question can be tough to answer. Sometimes it may be wise to hold the status quo. Other times the organization needs to be pushed (sometimes kicking and screaming) into a new era. When Alan Mulally became CEO of Ford, he and his team developed a global strategy called One Ford that optimized resources to improve vehicles and deliver stronger returns.[5]

These questions demand more than cookie-cutter responses; they challenge the leader to examine what the organization needs and what his or her motives are for pushing for change.

Think About...

What it takes to eliminate conflict on your team so that people can focus on issues rather than personalities.

Consider ways you can encourage people to collaborate more effectively.

What questions will you ask yourself when you are facing long odds? What will the answers tell you about yourself and the people on your team?

How will you keep your team motivated when working on demanding projects?

Perseverance = Truth + Determination

65. | Deliver a Reason to Be Urgent

LEADERS MUST DO TWO THINGS WHEN THEY MANAGE: provide a good reason for what they're doing and add a sense of urgency.

Let's break down reason and urgency into their fundamentals.

Reason is based upon logic, a deductive flow from A to B and so on. You start the flow of ideas with solid facts. You speak in terms of consequence, that is, what happens next and why. For example, we need to add an engineer to our team because we need someone who enjoys solving problems. With that engineer on board we will be able to do our own diagnostics. That will enable us to improve our delivery times as well as our quality ratings.

Urgency is rooted in an impetus for action, the need to do it now. You want to emphasize the need to move quickly and the importance of acting promptly. An example would be making a case for a new product. Your argument could be rooted in the fact that the competition is working on something similar and you want to capitalize on the first-mover advantage.

Reason and urgency are not mutually exclusive. That is, reason can be compelling and urgency does have consequence. But if you stand back and think about each separately it may give you a handle on structuring a fact-based argument that provides a strong basis for action.

The ability to persuade others is a chief requirement of effective leadership. The manager who can learn to balance his communications with the proper blend of reason (facts) and urgency (do it now) will be one who can mobilize others to his point of view.

Need + Reason + Action = Urgency

66. | Wield Power Gracefully When Making Decisions

IF YOU WANT TO LEAD OTHERS, you need to get comfortable with the concept of power.

Emerging leaders sometimes stumble over the use of power for one of two reasons. Either they are too comfortable with it and wield it ruthlessly, or they are so fearful of it they avoid it completely.

Decide when to power down. It's true that sometimes you can be more effective by not using your authority. Jeff Immelt, CEO of GE, once told the *New York Times* he had to tell people "You're doing it my way" between seven and twelve times annually.[6] If he did this only three times, the organization would lack discipline; if he did it eighteen times, good executives would flee.

Know when to apply power. While you want to push decision making to the front lines, there will be times when you need to make a big decision. Making that call will mean you have to exert power. So make the decision and communicate it so that everyone understands its implications and what they need to do to support it.

Follow through with power. Decision making is the first step. It is up to the leader to bring people together to implement the plan. When organizations fail, it's often because people end up doing their own thing— instead of the right thing. They become distracted by competing priorities and fail to follow through on their commitments as a consequence.

Leaders who use their power to make sure that decisions are executed in a timely fashion ensure that the initiative won't lose focus or momentum.

Think About...

How leaders should apply their power to achieve positive aims.

What is the link between urgency and power? In others words, do leaders sometimes overplay urgency simply because they have the power to do so? How will you avoid doing that?

Consider ways you can eliminate tasks to give people time to focus on what is important.

Consider a time when you used your authority and the outcome was not positive. What went wrong and what did you learn from the experience?

Power = Purposeful Authority

67. Hold the Platitudes

IF YOU VALUE YOUR PEOPLE, don't do it with words. Do it with your actions.

Stop pretending. Be straight with people; give them the big picture explanation of what is happening. For example, explain the opportunities and challenges facing the business and what the implications are for individual employees And if you don't know something, admit it, but try to find out—sooner rather than later so you can relay the news to your employees.

Encourage personal decision making. Give employees more control over how they do their jobs. Managers determine the "what to do," but when employees have a say in the way they do their job, they feel more engaged. Loss of control over one's fate is vexing in a downturn, but if employees feel they have some input into how they do their work, they feel more in control.

Invest in employees. Training and development are typically cut during down economies. That's too bad, because often the acquisition of new skills and the development of untapped talents are the factors that will help the company survive the downturn. Sometimes downturns bring lulls in the work flow. Use such time wisely by grooming your talent base.

> Leaders who value their employees demonstrate
> commitment through their actions.

• • • • • • •

68. | Use Your Senses to Hire

THINKING OF A JOB CANDIDATE in terms of how he or she might fit into the team is the best way to consider a new hire.

Consider the "sensory approach" that Rich Cho, who has been general manager of the NBA's Charlotte Bobcats as well as of the Portland Trailblazers, uses when evaluating talent for his team.

Eyes. Consider how the job candidate comports himself. Watch how he treats other interviewers, as well as administrative staff. A candidate who schmoozes with a bigwig but blows off a secretary shows a lack of courtesy. When evaluating internal candidates, look at how others treat him. Do they see him as a teammate or as an obstacle?

Ears. Listening to stories about a potential candidate is not the same as indulging in gossip. You are looking for insights about work ethic as well as ability to get along with others. Ask the candidate about accomplishments.

If the words *I did* appear more than *we did*, it may be an indication of someone who likes to play alone or believes she deserves special consideration. Find out from others how well the candidate gets along with them.

Numbers. It is perfectly acceptable to judge a potential employee or manager by what she has accomplished. Managers are measured by what they accomplish, so you want to quantify the returns. This is easy when judging sales talent or even line managers but more dicey when hiring someone in design or human resources. You need to develop metrics germane to the function that make sense. Look at what the individual achieved in terms of contributions that were implemented and succeeded.

The beauty of such an approach to talent evaluation is that it seeks to place the person in context, that is, how he or she performed in current and previous situations. It is by no means perfect. Hiring from the outside may be more risky than promoting from within, but both have their drawbacks. New hires must adapt to your culture, and may butt heads with others; managers from within an organization may be trapped by their culture, afraid to do new things.[7]

Thinking of a job candidate as a total person,
one with his own eyes, ears, and mind, is a good way
of helping that person to integrate into a new
organization or a new role.

69. | Hire for Character and Integrity

JUDGING CHARACTER IS NOT A MYSTERY; it is a matter of watching how a person interacts with others and the effect that individual has on others. A truism in drama is that character is action. The same holds for leadership. How an individual acts defines who he is.

Accomplishments merit attention, but it is always wise to peek behind the curtain to see how these successes were achieved. To do this, consider three questions:

How well does the individual work with others?
Teams need leaders who are willing to work with others. The ability to cooperate is essential to teamwork. From it can emerge collaboration that is essential to team success.

How does the individual deal with adversity?
Setbacks are inevitable. A leader must be one who can address an obstacle with a clear head. Knowing how to deal with adversity is a measure of a leader's ability to achieve.

How do others regard this individual? Everyone wants to be liked, but affinity comes second to respect. Respect is rooted in integrity and reinforced by competency and credibility.

Simple questions, yes, but their answers will give you insight into the character of the individual. Character is a reflection of integrity; it is the framework upon which a person's behavior is based.

Managers therefore may do well to tolerate an individual who exhibits quirky habits, as long as those quirks do not harm others or the team. And never should an employee (or manager) be allowed to cross ethical boundaries in business or in personal relations. Character matters.[8]

Managers who hire people without integrity imperil not only their teams but also the character of their organizations.

Think About...

Ways you demonstrate that actions speak louder than words when it comes to showing concern for employees and stakeholders.

Consider how you evaluate your job candidates. What are the three most important things you look for in a potential new employee?

Why are these factors important to you and your organization?

What are you doing to ensure that these factors are considered?

Character = Integrity + Action

70. | What You Need to Ask About Your Company

LEADERS REVEAL THEIR VALUES on a daily basis. The best work hard to make certain that everyone in the company understands those values. Start by asking three questions:

Do people know what the organization stands for? Take the lofty vision or mission statements. Are they nice-sounding words that describe what the organization does? Or are they nice-sounding words that look good on posters but not in real life? If there is a disconnect between vision and values, it is hard for people to believe that the company stands for anything. When that happens, people go through the motions on matters of character. They do not automatically cheat or lie but do not go out of their way to serve their customers or even each other.

Do people believe that ethics in the organization matter? People know that legal transgressions will get them in trouble. But what about the guy who climbs over others to get the big promotion? Do bosses who demean others, and throw their people under the proverbial bus, get rewarded? When these things happen, employees quickly realize that ethical behavior is not valued; statements about ethics are mere platitudes.

What am I doing to set the right example? This covers standing up for the team, focusing on the issues, and getting things done. It also includes the people-development side of management, coaching and mentoring, and pushing for career and professional opportunities for your people. Respected managers are known for doing these things.

Never assume people know what your company stands for. Make time to teach them.

• • • • • • •

71. | Three Ways to Execute Better

VERY OFTEN ORGANIZATIONS FAIL because their leaders fail to execute.

The irony of poor execution is that it is preventable. Here's how to do it:

Make execution a priority. How many times have you heard a senior executive, when faced with a setback, say that he or she is returning to fundamentals? It makes good sense, but the intention fades as soon as the heat is off. The challenge is to keep the heat on, to continue to execute with urgency. You create urgency by driving home the importance of continuing to perform at a high level. You create metrics and hold yourself and your team to them. This is not fun, but it is a way to ensure that quality and service levels remain high.

Visit the workplace. Good executives are those who do not rely solely upon monthly reports or what their direct reports tell them. These managers spend time with people on the front lines who make the product or deliver the service. They ask good questions and they listen. Such executives engage with their employees to find new and better ways to do things so that employees and customers benefit.

Follow through. When managers are pressed for time, the first task to be eliminated is often checking on the work flow. Good execution relies upon constant monitoring. Follow-through means contacting customers to check on product and service performance. Follow-through also dictates that you provide your team with the resources you promised them.[9]

Improving execution begins with those
with most responsibility—leaders!

72. | Step Back to Lead

IT IS A LEADER'S RESPONSIBILITY to provide direction. But sometimes leaders need to *take* direction. Leaders often have a hard time knowing when to let others step forward, but no leader can do everything, nor should she.

So when should leaders step back and let others lead? Here are three questions to help you make that decision:

What are you trying to achieve in your leadership role? Leaders must always be looking downfield, scanning for new opportunities and emerging challenges. By focusing too much on the here and now, you end up managing details, but not leading people. Effective administration is fundamental to good order, yes, but a manager who gets so immersed in minutiae is failing to apply her talents to the betterment of the organization.

Is this project the best use of your time? Before you tackle a project, consider whether it merits the investment of your time. Meeting with customers and employees, helping to solve problems, listening to your team, and providing guidance to others are part of what leaders do.

Do you trust others to step forward? By stepping back, leaders are not stepping out. They must always remain fully in control of what they are responsible for: decision making, direction, and motivation.[10]

Leaders need to engage on those issues that require their direct involvement. Otherwise, they should ease off and let the people they have hired do their jobs.

Think About...

Ways you can improve execution in the context of your organizational mission.

Ask yourself how you can link individual contributions to the fulfillment of the organizational mission.

Consider two specific actions that you must take to improve execution in your organization.

What can you do to ensure that your people have the time and resources they need to do their jobs right?

$$\text{Execution} = \frac{\text{Attention} + \text{Diligence}}{\text{Work}}$$

73. | Don't Give In to Defeatism

DEFEATISM IS THE ABSENCE OF HOPE. It indicates that the system is broken. Giving up the ghost may be an option, but it's not the only option. Consider the following:

Bury the dead. Reality demands facing the truth. Quite simply it is the acknowledgment that what we do is not enough. We may have been rolling in the good times, but now our customers cannot afford what we offer, or discover they can do without. Find out the truth and accept it. At the same time, make time to close the chapter. Remember the good things, as well as the good contributors. Mourn what you have lost.

Resolve to move forward. You have a choice. Push out or push on. You can argue for both, but if you decide to go on, you need to resolve to think positively. A colleague of mine, Kathy Macdonald, argues that managers must give their people the "illusion of reality." What Macdonald means by that is managers must often take things into their own hands. They cannot always wait for direction from on high. Therefore, in the absence of direction, move forward. Make things happen that are consistent with organizational vision and mission.

Think renewal. Because things are so dire, it is time to do things differently. Nothing should be shielded from scrutiny. Consider every step of every operation to think about how to do it more effectively and efficiently. Cost-cutting is not the answer; reengineering value is. That starts with the way you manage. Discover ways to do things differently.

Rejuvenation may require that people shift roles and responsibilities. Give younger employees more responsibilities. Offer veteran employees more developmental assignments that prepare the next generation to lead. Every organization will need to discover its own ways to rethink its management principles.

Ignore defeatism at your peril. Acknowledge its existence so you can rise above it rather than surrendering to it.

74. | Generate Enthusiasm About the Work

GENERATING ENTHUSIASM, or passion, for what you do is essential.

Ultimately, instilling passion for the work is more than an exercise in rah-rah; it is a search for meaning and significance. So how can you cultivate passion for work in others and do it in ways that have significance? Here are some suggestions.

Focus on the positive. Passion in leaders can be palpable; you know in an instant that the executive cares about the company. In my experience, those senior leaders who stroll through the halls with a nod or good word to say to all are those executives who get things done. They regularly meet with employees and customers, vendors and investors, getting to know issues and concerns.

Address the negatives. Passionate leaders are not wide-eyed dreamers; they know the score, precisely because they spend so much time out of their offices. They see firsthand what is working and what is not, and because they have a relationship with people in all levels of the company, they can more readily mobilize employees to solve problems.

Set high expectations. Those who care about the work and set a high standard challenge others to do the same, but they should remember to balance their

approach—knowing to sometimes ease up on workloads
but never on expectations.

Radiating passion is no excuse for ignoring
attention to the fundamentals.

• • • • • • •

75. | Lead Like a Salesperson

LEADERS CAN LEARN something from the way good salespeople connect with their customers.

Link to aspiration. Appeal to one thing that many of us crave: legacy. Effective salespeople, and leaders, connect to people's aspirations for something more, something bigger than themselves. If you need to generate enthusiasm for a new initiative or product launch, focus on how much better the company will be when the transformation occurs or the new product drops. Savvy leaders make it known that such good things can occur only when talented employees join together to make good things happen.

Address the negatives. There is always resistance in the sales process. From a transactional viewpoint, employees (like customers) may prefer the status quo because even if things are uncomfortable, they are known. You can't ignore the negatives—deal with them head-on. Acknowledge them and defuse them with an effective argument. Also, never overpromise.

Sometimes it's possible to **Turn negatives into positives.** For example, reorganizations always provoke thoughts of downsizing. Acknowledge that notion and then either dismiss it because it is untrue or acknowledge its validity. After that, talk about how the reorganization will cause short-term pain in the interest of creating long-term gain, like increased opportunities for individuals to maximize their skills and achieve more for themselves and the company.

Sell from the top. When employees see their leader selling to a customer, or pushing an initiative through the organization, it sends a message that no one is too big or too important to engage in salesmanship. Any member of an organization should consider selling—or more realistically, promoting—the work of the company. Do this by talking up the work your organization does, what good products it makes, and how those products help make the lives of others better.

Be careful: Too much salesmanship can appear to be slickness. Avoid this by tempering your enthusiasm with periodic reality checks and by listening to stakeholders.

Think About...

Actions you must take to ensure that people know that you value them as contributors who are vital to the success of the organization.

Consider how you "connect the dots" between what an employee does and how the organization performs.

How can you enable direct reports to take the lead on specific projects? What will you do to support their efforts?

What specific actions can you take to generate enthusiasm about the work?

Commitment = Engagement + Enthusiasm

76. Five Ways to Connect with Those Who Can't Stand You

AS A LEADER YOU WILL sometimes find yourself in need of help in learning how to reach those who may not want to hear you.

Be accessible. Understand how the people you are speaking to think. Be available to speak to them informally.

Know your facts. When we feel passionate about the issue, there is a tendency to rely on the emotion of the argument rather than the business case. Make certain you know the business case.

Tell a story. Weave stories into your argument. It makes your case more understandable as well as more heartfelt.

Avoid getting into the gutter. Stick to your argument and don't throw mud at your opposition. Bottom line: It is important to stay calm as well as to treat those who disagree with you as colleagues, not enemies. Even if they hurl invectives at you, keep your cool.

Appeal to the "better angels." Getting backing for an initiative requires the support of more than a few people; a leader must bring people together by reaching out to those who may disagree and commending them on their values. Relate their values to yours as you seek common ground.

You may not win your battle, but you will
establish yourself as one who can advocate
with a clear head and in a composed manner.
That will win you points in the long run.

Think About...

How you can communicate your point of view in
ways that demonstrate your open-mindedness.

Connection = Open Mind + Willing Spirit

77. | When the Going Gets Tough, Lead

PEOPLE ADMIRE STRONG LEADERSHIP, especially in times of crisis.

Nothing instills clarity like informed communications. Honest communications demonstrate that you're a straight shooter, one who can be trusted.

Explain how the crisis affects your business.
Call a meeting with your staff and explain how the current crisis affects or does not affect your business. Is it too soon to know how it will affect your company? Admit that and then keep people informed of any new developments.

Focus on the work.
The best way to ensure job security is to continue to do what you are asked to do. Managers and employees need to focus on execution—getting things done right, on time, and on budget.[11]

To quote legendary basketball coach John Wooden's maxim, "Don't let what you cannot do interfere with what you can do."

78. | When Things Go Wrong

FAILURE TO RESPOND TO A CRISIS is a failure of leadership. Knowing when to become involved is a component of the response.

When a crisis strikes, leaders need to do three things:

Be seen. You can tell if a leader is up to the job when trouble strikes. If a top boss stays hidden, or cloistered with staff and unavailable to employees, you know he is not right for the job.

Be heard. We want to know what's in our leaders' minds; they need to let us know what they are thinking through their words and their actions. If they do not articulate a message, an information vacuum develops, allowing rumors to proliferate.

Be there. This is the tough one. Being there means being part of the action, becoming actively engaged in the process of stemming the crisis or putting the organization back together after the crisis has passed.

The cold, hard reality of crisis management is that crises are unpredictable. Seldom do they follow a script. Leaders need to be active and engaged whenever they are called upon, and they must demonstrate a sense of calmness and control. A leader who withdraws from the fray or seems hopelessly lost sends the worst kind of signals. This breeds fear, from which no good can come.[12]

No leader can stop a hurricane, or the aftereffects of a product recall, but he or she can step up and exert command over the situation. This comes from knowing the circumstances, trusting in the judgment of colleagues, and making decisions deliberately and decisively. We call that leadership.

• • • • • • •

79. | Develop a Crisis Plan

CRISES MAY STRIKE at any time. The challenge is to prepare yourself to lead when the worst happens. Here are some tips on how to manage yourself and your message when the heat is on.

Prepare yourself. The only thing you can be sure of about a crisis is that it will likely occur when you least expect it. You cannot prepare for the specifics, but you can coach yourself on how to respond. Just as companies have crisis plans, so too, must executives. Think about what you would say and how you would say it. Practicing forms of meditation will help you learn to stay calm. Nothing will prepare you for the severity of what occurs, but

thinking about how you would respond in advance—
before any crisis occurs—is good practice.

Plan your message. Think about what you will say.
Do not approach the podium and expect to wing it.
Do an outline and jot down thoughts for talking points.
You can even write up a situation report as an opening
statement. Huddle with your staff to get their ideas. Be
collaborative in accepting ideas from others.

Get right to the point. When you take the podium,
address the key issue immediately. Acknowledge the
severity of the situation and the damage. For example, if
there was a plant fire, lead with the fire and then speak of
injuries. Express sympathy for victims and their families.
You might also talk about what it will mean to production
to lose the plant. But save the details for later; be clear and
concise in your prepared remarks.

Take questions. Here is where good leaders shine.
Invite the audience (reporters or employees) to ask questions. Be as candid as you can. Also, invite subject-matter
experts to join you on the stage to speak to their specific
areas of expertise. If you don't know the answer, admit it
and promise to give a response as soon as possible. By
taking questions, you demonstrate that you are in charge
and are able to respond to the breaking news situation.

Be accountable for what you are doing. A senior
leader is responsible for how the organization responds to
the crisis. Make it clear that you are in charge. People
want to know there is someone in authority who is managing the issues and their consequences. Such authority

does not guarantee positive results, but it does give people assurance that someone knows what is going on.[13]

Preparing yourself to lead when things go bad is the first lesson of crisis management.

Think About...

How you will ensure that when crisis strikes you will be in charge.

What is the first step you will take in developing a crisis plan? Who will you enlist to help you?

What steps will you take personally to ensure that you maintain your equilibrium and remain calm in the face of adversity? Is there an individual you know who has experienced such difficulties from whom you can learn? What questions will you ask this person?

How will you regenerate enthusiasm in the workplace after the crisis recedes? What will you do first? What expectations do you have for success?

$$\text{Preparation} = \frac{\text{Foresight} + \text{Planning}}{\text{Practicality}}$$

80. | Cut Out the Doom and Gloom

LEADERS NEED TO CHOOSE THEIR WORDS CAREFULLY.

Striking the right tone is a matter of understanding context and your people, and choosing words that address a crisis realistically but do not induce fear. Here are some suggestions for crafting your message.

Think ahead. If your company is experiencing serious difficulty, consider how you will explain it. Do not use words like "stupid" and "idiotic" when referring to senior managers. You may feel like saying them, but avoid doing so. Use words such as "challenged" or "unaware." Blaming individuals is good for blowing off steam, but it is not good for instilling faith in the company.

Pause before you speak. When you are asked a question about the business, pause before you answer. The pause radiates calmness. It demonstrates that you are in control. You may not be, but you want your team to believe that you are holding things together. The pause also gives you time to gather your thoughts as well as to cool down if you are feeling overwrought.

Avoid hyperbole. Just as you would not pour gasoline over an open flame, do not use words like "disastrous," "catastrophe," and "meltdown." Such words escalate tensions; a leader's job is to de-escalate tension. Use words like "serious," "tough," and "wrongheaded." These make your point without raising an employee's blood pressure.

Convey urgency. Tough times demand tough talk, but make sure you talk in ways that focus on what people *need to do* rather than what they *cannot do*. That is, talk specifically about how employees can do more with fewer resources by trimming less valuable tasks.

Avoid blame; instead, accept ownership for the things you can control, like your work ethic and attitude.

Words + Tone = Meaning

81. When Speaking in Front of a Hostile Audience

NOT EVERYONE WILL BE RECEPTIVE to your leadership message. If you know you must speak in front of an audience that may not be receptive to your message, do it with style.

Be brief. Keep prepared remarks direct and on point.

Argue the case, not personalities. Focus on facts, not on the person asking you questions. The person asking questions may not be likable, but treat him with respect.

Act professional as well as patient. Pay attention to what others say. Even when you disagree, maintain your composure.

Never, ever take the bait. Elected officials will look for a way to trip you up. Do not give it to them. Defend yourself and your company, but never seem defensive.

Radiate confidence. Act like you have been doing this for a while. Appear relaxed and in control of your emotions. It may even be appropriate to smile, especially when making small talk.

Such public appearances may seem a waste of time, but as a senior leader it is your obligation to your company—and important to your credibility—to appear.

These rules are simple, so simple, in fact, they might seem insulting. But that is just the point. Failure to abide by them may insult your reputation. It makes you look bad and your company look worse.

Think About...

How you can develop a key message that sums up your leadership point of view.

Consider a time when you went off message because you lost your cool. What was the reaction of others? What will you do differently?

Think of ways you can maintain self-control when others are losing theirs.

Give an example of how you will dispel gloom and refocus on opportunities.

Composure = Calmness + Control

82. | **Put Principle over Policy**

Principles are the core values that shape a leader's outlook and frame the purpose of the organization that he or she leads. Such core values may include honesty, integrity, and respect for human dignity.

By contrast, policies are practices that a leader and the organization follow. Both principles and policies may be rooted in core values—they often are—but they are not the same. Principles, because they are central to belief, should not be altered; policies can be changed because of circumstance.

A leader's responsibility is to do right by the people he or she leads. Holding to values and principles is a matter of integrity. Changing policy to help the organization address changing times and therefore be better positioned to serve in the future is a good thing.

83. | Build Common Cause

THE JOB OF A LEADER IS TO BRING PEOPLE TOGETHER for common cause.

You can build common cause four ways:

1. **Demonstrate the vision and couple it with urgency.** Coming up with vision is important, but giving it impetus in order to fulfill it is harder. This is where executives need to drive home the mission with their communications. They also need to challenge their direct reports to do the same by translating the vision into day-to-day action steps so people know what is expected of them.

2. **Hold people accountable for their actions.** Expectations are relatively simple to set. The challenge arises in following through on them. When the stakes are high, managers who do not follow through will be transferred to other jobs, or asked to leave. Do this a few times and people get the message pretty quickly. Those at the top are not exempt from review. Accountability applies to everyone.

3. **Insist on localized decision making.** Employees want the freedom to express their point of view on key issues. No organization can survive for long if everyone thinks and acts the same way.

Savvy leaders build in room for pushback. You need to encourage employees at every level to think for themselves and make appropriate decisions that complement the organization's vision, mission, and values. This allows for employees to contribute with their brains but keeps the organization's spine (mission) intact.

4. **Celebrate the outcomes.** Managing a large-scale enterprise is tough, and when the organization is challenged to change, it is even harder. Employees lose focus pretty quickly. That is why those at the top need to acknowledge the milestones and, more important, recognize those who have helped the organization achieve those milestones.[14]

If people in the middle, and on the front lines, do not believe in the directives, they will not follow through on them. That's where a strong leader, coupled with a robust management system, is a must.

Think About...

How you will demonstrate that collaboration is important to organizational success.

Consider a time when you stood up for principle. What happened? How did others react? Would you do it again and why?

Give an example of how you will communicate common cause throughout your organization.

What steps will you take to ensure that everyone knows the mission and their role in fulfilling it?

Common Cause = Purpose + Engagement

84. | Defuse Discord

DISAGREEMENTS ARE FINE; discord is not. Disagreements typically center on ideas; discord focuses on people. Here is how to defuse it.

Diagnose the root cause. Find out why coworkers are in conflict with one another. Often the roots of the discord lie in things that occurred long ago. One person may feel slighted because his ideas were rejected by his boss whereas those of a coworker were accepted. Another might feel that he is not receiving his fair share of time and resources to complete a project. Still another may feel overlooked when she did not receive an expected promotion. Such issues, when not addressed promptly, can fester over time and can breed hostility.

Stay high and dry. If a boss is responsible for problems, he should acknowledge them and apologize. Look for ways to improve the situation through further discussion and dialogue. However, if the roots of discord occurred before you were manager, acknowledge the hurt feelings but do not take sides. In other words, don't swim in the water under the bridge; walk over the bridge. Failure to do so simply allows individuals to wallow in their misery.

Defuse the conflict. Make it clear that cooperation is mandatory. Managers who allow employees to act on grudges are giving the aggrieved more reasons to be disagreeable. Establish a no-tolerance policy for disagreements over people and personalities. Hold everyone, including yourself, accountable to that standard.

Find common ground. People in conflict have no difficulty identifying differences; those differences are what fuel their disagreements. The challenge for a manager is to get the conflicting parties to put aside those differences. The best way to do that is to identify common values. For example, both parties will want the company to succeed; that is a common purpose. Make it clear that their discord is destroying that value proposition and insist that they stop it.

Follow through. Just because you have gotten people to stop shouting at each other does not mean they are working together. Continue to monitor the situation. Watch for warning signs among former combatants such as angry expressions, lack of eye contact, and the silent treatment. Affirm individuals' contributions but at the same time make it clear that cooperation is required. Those who fail to treat coworkers with respect will be removed from the team.

Disagreement over issues is a sign of a healthy workplace. Discord over people issues is a sign of dysfunction. Managers need to encourage behaviors that do not marginalize individuals.

Think About...

Ways that you will emphasize that you value open and honest dialogue with your direct reports.

How will you ensure that when tensions rise you focus on the root cause rather than its symptoms?

Consider why it is important that you remain above the fray when tensions rise.

Give an example of how you will welcome feedback from others.

Honest Dialogue = Candor + Truth

85. | Right a Wrong

WHEN PEOPLE IN THE ORGANIZATION BREAK THE RULES, it falls to you to set things straight. A leader's physical presence as well as his personal involvement demonstrates that business as usual is over.

Address the wrongs. When scandal strikes, organizations want to protect themselves. The best thing they can do, however, is come clean. Running from the problem rather than confronting it only makes things worse.

Make amends. Apologize, then right the wrong. Do it quickly and efficiently. Do not err on the side of caution; err on the side of the victim. Remember always that your company made the mistake. It is your responsibility to fix it.

Let the wronged vent. When people are hurt, either from services you render or a product you offer, you need to make restitution. Part of that process should involve more than an apology. Let the victims speak out. Listen to the pain your company has caused. It is not pleasant, but it is necessary for healing.

Be engaged. When trouble brews within your organization it may not be enough to stand back and let others do the work. Sometimes it is necessary to put yourself into the front lines and stay there.

The lesson for leaders: remain engaged. You cannot control the situation but you can control how you respond to it. Sometimes that may be the only hope an organization has.

Think About...

Ways you can create a work climate in which people can admit mistakes and make amends.

How will you make it safe for people to raise concerns when they feel they have been wronged?

Consider a time when you made amends for a mistake you made at work. What was the reaction of others? What did you learn from the experience?

Apology = Acknowledgment + Amends

86. Questions to Help You Coach Your Employees

A LEADER'S PRIORITY IS TO HELP his employees do their jobs better. Coaching plays a key role in this enablement process.

When writing fiction, novelist Ellis Avery asks herself questions about her characters' motives and intentions. Two of these questions, with slight adaptation, work for managers seeking to develop the talents of their employees.[15]

What does my employee want? This question uncovers motivation. Some employees want to be promoted; others want opportunities for development. Many want the opportunity to earn more. Virtually all employees strive for recognition, which is a basic human desire. It is up to the manager to discover an employee's motivators so that he or she can speak to the employee in ways that are relevant and meaningful.

What is stopping my employee from achieving her objectives? All of us—high achievers included— have blind spots. It is up to the manager to identify not only strengths but also things that are holding the employee back. It could be poor communications or failure to hold oneself accountable.

And here is a question unique to managers: **What can I do to help my employee become successful?** The manager needs to be there for his employee. Sometimes he will serve to challenge the employee by giving her stretch goals. Other times he will act as a cheerleader, helping the employee overcome an obstacle.

Keep in mind that the coach's job is never to do the employee's work for her; it is to help the individual recognize what she must do in order to succeed.

These questions are best handled in regularly scheduled sessions. The tone should be affirmative as well as conversational. The manager as coach demonstrates belief in the employee's abilities and does what he can to help her achieve.

Leaders who coach are those who treat
their employees as individuals and
regard them as contributors.

87. | Buck Up the Team

FINDING WAYS TO CHEER THE TEAM is a manager's job. Doing so when the going gets tough builds a foundation for greater trust.

Here are some suggestions, all beginning with the letter *A*.

Advise. Share what you know about the business, even when the news is not good. Make yourself willing to listen to your employees' concerns. Share your expertise as well as yourself. That means providing advice about the work as well as insight into improving performance. So much of management today is coaching, that is, putting the people in the right slots and then helping them achieve. Just because business is down, spirits need not be. Managers fight negativity by affirming the contributions their employees make.

Act. Managers must do something. Leaders act for the good of the team. This means that you need to consider ways you can help the team do its work. Provide additional resources when possible. If not, pitch in and help. Acting for the team also means spreading kindness. Mark milestones of achievement. On an individual basis, look for employees who may be struggling. Perhaps they need an extra hand or need to be paired with a colleague. Additional training may be in order. This additional help should be temporary; chronic underperformance means the person is not in the right job.

Admonish. Pay attention to what employees are saying as well as not saying. Grousing and grumbling are part of the everyday workplace, but if such words begin to encroach on behavior, the manager must step in. Complaints will be accepted, but complaining will not. The former may be justified; the latter is not because it affects behavior. The manager needs to keep the team focused on the work and on the goals.

When the chips are down, the leader
should be the first one to pick them up.

Think About...

What you can do to spread confidence throughout your organization.

Think of a time you spent coaching an employee. What did you do to help the employee succeed?

What will you do next time your team fails to meet an agreed-upon objective? What will you do to correct them? What will you do to cheer them on?

Give an example of how you will demonstrate that individual contributions add up to team success.

Team Success = Collaboration + Commitment

88. | Lead with Passion

PASSION GETS YOU UP IN THE MORNING; it is the fuel that drives you to immerse yourself in your work and deliver results.

To demonstrate passion:

Set high goals. People who love what they do love to push to see how high and how well they can fly. By setting stretch objectives, you push motivated people to do their best. The pursuit dovetails with their passion.

Stoke the fires. Give frequent feedback so people know where they stand. When folks get off track, show them the way back so they can apply their passion toward meeting the needs of the team.

Measure results. Passionate people love to know how they are doing and what it means. Show them that what they do matters in terms of gains against goals. And whatever the measurement, broadcast it.

Use passion as a lever to help individuals
and teams do their jobs better.

89. | Lead with Compassion

COMPASSION IS WHAT YOU EXTEND TO OTHERS; it is the manifestation of caring and concern.

To nurture compassion:

Coach frequently. Management is a process of enabling others to succeed, specifically putting them into positions where they can do so. Provide them with guidance. This is the compassion equivalent of "stoke the fires."

Put people first. Look for ways to put this concept into action. Insist on people-friendly HR policies related to sick leave and child and elder care. Consider flexible schedules. Look for ways to accommodate those who want to work part-time, such as parents with young children.

Support volunteerism. Make it known that your organization will donate time and effort to community service. Perhaps it is a local school or maybe a family shelter or a multiplicity of assistance efforts. Some organizations provide paid leave for people engaged in the community's volunteer activities.

Compassion is the outward demonstration
of feeling and care from one person to another.

Think About...

Why it is necessary for employees to be passionate about their work.

How should a leader encourage a sense of pride in the workplace?

Give an example of how you demonstrated compassion for an employee.

Why is it appropriate to balance passion for work with compassion for people? What happens when that occurs? Why? And what can we learn from it?

Approachability = Passion/Compassion

• • • • • • •

90. | How You Can Add More Value to Your Organization

VERY OFTEN WE ARE BLIND to what we could be doing differently. So we need to adopt a fresh perspective on our contributions to the organization.

Toward that end, here are three questions:

How am I adding value to the organization?

Consider what you are doing now. Draw up a list of your responsibilities and then compare them to a list of actions you have taken. Do they match? For example, if you are a vice president for finance and you are spending time balancing the books, you are not operating at your level. Likewise, if you are a sales executive and you spend all of your time in the office and no time with your people or your customers, it may be an issue. Reconcile your actions with your role.

How am I encouraging others to add value?

Leaders need to bring out the best in their teams. What actions are you taking to delegate more responsibility to others? Are you providing clear expectations and following up to see that people have the resources they need to do their jobs? Looking down the road, how are you planning for others to assume your role or roles of other senior leaders? These are big questions, and all of them have an impact on value.

What could I be doing differently? Tough question. While you may know how you are spending your time, you need to consider whether your activities are the best use of your time. For example, senior leaders need to disengage from tactics and work strategically. They need to delegate tactics to others in order to have time to think and act strategically. Part of acting strategically may mean spending more time with customers. Or it may involve networking with colleagues in your field but outside of your company in order to gain a fresh perspective on your business.

Doing things differently is not always necessary, but leaders need to remain open to the possibility of change so they can provide the guidance their organization requires.

Think About...

Ways you can add value to your organization.

Give an example of how you reconsidered your activities in ways that led you to do things differently. How did you learn to think more strategically? How did you learn to delegate tasks to others?

Consider ways you can learn from colleagues inside and outside your business. What specific questions will you ask them about gaining a new perspective on your role within your organization?

Leadership Balance = Stability + Flexibility

91. | Are Your Employees Listening?

COMMUNICATION ISN'T JUST about what management says; it's also about how employees hear.

Here are some ways to check whether your message is being heard.

Test the message. After a key message is developed, test it with employees. Do this informally, one-on-one or at selected staff meetings. Make sure to get the reactions of some employees you suspect will be among the hardest to win over. Solicit their ideas for changing the message, or parts of the message. Allowing these employees to shape the message will accomplish two goals: first, it will improve your message, making it more likely to be successful; second, it will make your harshest critics more likely to feel a part of the communication process and, ideally, will bring them on board as messengers.

Incentivize the process. Whether you convene a series of meetings to deliver your message in person, or rely on electronic or other means of communication, there will be people who skip the meetings or delete the emails. Once you start rolling out your message, use basic incentives to induce people to listen. Make it a breakfast or lunch meeting and offer food to make people more likely to show up. If you're sending out a new policy over email, request a read-receipt and say you'll be giving coupons or small gift cards (say, $5

redeemable at a nearby coffee shop) to the first X
number of people who read it.

Audit for results. After the communication cycle is
complete, follow up. Were there people who skipped the
briefing meetings? Set up one-on-ones with them to make
sure they get the message. And check in with all your
employees to ask if they have questions about the changes,
or feedback on your communication efforts. If you have
a large organization, this can be done with an open-ended
survey. Structure it so that you can capture how your
message was received emotionally as well as how well
its content was understood. If audit results are not
acceptable, you may want to conduct another wave of
communications.

Resistance to communication is a symptom of
organizational dysfunction; it is a sign that not
everyone is on board. The sooner managers address
these situations, the greater the likelihood of
solving the issues and getting people on board.

Think About...

Ways you can improve communication in your workplace.

What steps will you take to ensure messages are heard? How will you check for understanding?

What can you do to ensure that you set the right example when it comes to listening more attentively?

Communication ≅ Team Effort

● ● ● ● ● ● ●

92. | Four Ways to Reverse a Decision

SOMETIMES A LEADER MAY reverse a key decision or hold fast to the chosen course. Knowing what to do, and when, defines a leader's legacy.

Examining a decision in context is essential to determining its efficacy. Asking four questions will help a leader gain perspective.

Why is this decision important? Big decisions require deliberation over time. Typically part of the equation involves testing assumptions, as in, "What is the cost of not doing what we propose doing?" Revisiting why a decision was made is a good first step because it will confirm why you did what you did. Sound decisions affirm the organizational mission.

Who benefits from the decision? There are winners and losers in every decision because decisions provoke change. Consequences of the decision may mean some people gain power and influence; others may lose it. Many more may suffer inconvenience. Resistance is to be expected; how to deal with resistance is a measure of leadership. It may require more active participation by the leader to ensure that everyone pulls together for the good of the organization.

What is the cost of reversing the decision? There are risks in reversing a significant decision, especially if time and resources have been invested in its implementation. This can make the organization look unfocused, even wishy-washy. At the same time, pulling back might be prudent because it will save the company from throwing good money after bad or alienating stakeholders.

What is best for the organization? The challenge leaders face every day is doing what the organization needs them to do. When a decision proves unpopular, it may make sense to hold the course, because the long-term gain outweighs the short-term pain. We see this often with corporate reorganizations.[16]

There is one area in which leaders cannot
reverse course: integrity. You can change policy, but
you cannot compromise principle. The former is
transactional; the latter is fundamental.

Think About...

How you might reverse a decision in order to
adjust to changing circumstances.

Consider a time when your organization reversed
a major decision. What were the consequences?
What did you learn from the experience?

What steps can you take to minimize the risks
when a decision must be reversed? What will you
tell your stakeholders—specifically customers and
employees?

How will you ensure that the organization benefits
when a decision is reversed?

Decision = Consequence

93. Managing When You Cannot Disclose Information

IT'S ONE OF THE TOUGHEST SITUATIONS A MANAGER CAN FACE: You have information that affects the job status of your employees but you can't disclose it.

Although many organizations strive for transparency when it comes to mergers and acquisitions (as well as corporate reorganizations), very often managers are privy to details but ordered to keep silent.

Focusing on the positive does not mean spinning fairy tales or speaking "corporatese." It does mean being candid. Here's how.

Keep everyone in the loop. Promise to reveal what you can about the pending news when you can reveal it. If you can dispel the gloom (job cuts) then do so. But if you cannot, remind people that they will be the first to know.

Answer questions respectfully. Employees will want to know what it means to them and will ask questions. Be patient. If your livelihood were at risk, you'd ask questions, too.

Do not wait for new news. Take a cue from first-responder commanders. In the wake of disasters, they issue regular bulletins about the status of rescue operations. Even when they do not have anything new to add, they issue a statement, or appear before the media to answer questions. In such instances, there is no such thing as overcommunication.

Invite positive suggestions. A manager in the middle cannot guarantee the status of his department, but sometimes he can be proactive in saving it. That is, he or she can position the good work the team does in ways that demonstrate the value of the team as well as that of its individual contributors.

None of us likes uncertainty, but the best way to deal with it is to acknowledge it. Avoiding the issue only raises doubts that can paralyze productivity.

• • • • • • •

94. | Let Your Face Show You Are in Charge

LEADERS CAN SOMETIMES COMMUNICATE MORE without words than with them. What matters is poise and conviction.

A leader need not always use words to convey meaning; nonverbal cues often say more than words can ever do. Unfortunately, too often nonverbal cues are displayed to the wrong effect; that is, they communicate distraction, disregard, or even distaste. Those in charge, especially those in very senior positions, must be careful not only with their words but also with their body language. Here are some suggestions.

Relax your facial muscles. It makes you look more approachable, and as such you will be able to better connect with your colleagues. (You can practice relaxing your facial muscles by looking in a mirror. This is not vanity; it's good sense.)

Invite inspection. Ask a trusted colleague to watch your facial expressions and your posture during a meeting, particularly a meeting in which there will be intense discussions. If you look bored or irritated, or if you are slumped in your seat looking out the window, you are sending a message that you would rather be elsewhere. If your face bears a severe expression, you may be telegraphing irritation. Be conscious that people are not only listening to what you say, but also watching how you carry yourself when you say it.

Don't blow off steam. In some cultures, notably Native American and Scandinavian, the person at the top says very little, often speaking last on important issues. Business leaders can also encourage subordinates to speak first and freely; interject only when you have something of real substance to add. When the fur is flying, what gets people's attention is quiet confidence. Don't raise your voice. Instead, once you have people's attention, speak calmly and with conviction.

Nothing radiates power like controlled emotions
when everyone else is shouting at each other.

Think About...

Ways you use your communications to keep people
up-to-date and informed on important issues.

Consider what you will do when you may have
information that because of reasons of corporate
confidentiality you cannot disclose. How will you
handle the situation?

When you are permitted to discuss what you had
previously been told to keep in confidence, what
will you do first? How will you maintain the trust
of your employees?

Give an example of a situation in which you
projected an image of being composed and in
control of your emotions. How did others react?
What did you learn from the experience?

Transparency = Openness + Trust

95. | Why Leaders Use Stories

LEADERS USE STORIES to dramatize urgency and humanize events in ways that produce greater understanding. There are several reasons for doing this.

To inform. We all want the facts, but if a leader wants the facts to matter, he needs to add a little seasoning. Stories can take raw data and give it life. For example, why not use a spreadsheet to tell a story about rising sales, or declining quality? Use the data to make your points. Then, flesh out that explanation with stories about the effect on individuals, teams, and the company as a whole.

To involve. If you need to get people on your side, you need to involve them in the process. You need to engage their interest. For example, if an executive needs to persuade people to support an initiative, she can describe how the initiative will benefit the customer but also emphasize how it will improve the lot of employees, too. (More customers, more sales, more revenues, more jobs, more opportunities for promotion, etc.)

To inspire. Employees become jaded; there is only so much "importance" they can absorb, even when their jobs are at stake, so it falls to leaders to find ways to inspire their teams. Stories are the ideal vehicle for inspiring people because successful stories can dramatize the human condition.

Inspirational stories give sustenance in times of travail. They communicate the can-do spirit in ways that touch our hearts and lift our spirits.

• • • • • • •

96. | Tell Your Story with Impact

LEADERS WHO TELL GOOD STORIES follow five basic rules.

Know your message. When it comes to persuasion we resist being told what to think but we are open to explanations of why we must think it. Savvy preachers use this technique on Sundays. Good stories have more than a point of view; they have a message. As such they are tools of persuasion. Consider what you want others to do and why you want them to do it. That is your message.

Find the right example. Look for what people around you are doing that relates to your point of view. If you want to persuade people to adopt safety standards, tell the story of what happened when someone did not follow protocol. If you want to demonstrate the benefits of a new process, use a story to explain how an individual would benefit.

Weave your narrative. It is best to use real-life examples. Talk about what an employee did to ensure safety or how a team adopted a new process and achieved improved results. Tie the employee's exemplary performance to a narrative by following strong story structure. Describe the situation. Talk about what happened. Close with the benefits pitch.

Support with facts. Using a narrative approach doesn't mean you can't use facts. Weave them into your narrative, or begin or end your story with them. At the same time, humanize them by relating their impact on individuals. That is, a 10 percent cut in our budget means we have to reduce travel expenses. Or a 15 percent increase in revenue means we can open a new facility.

Convey passion. You don't need to go overboard, but you do need to demonstrate your conviction. Do this through your choice of words—ones that draw pictures. And do it through your delivery—raising your voice on a key point, pausing for emphasis, and following through with well-paced flow.

Practicing the principles of strong narratives
enables leaders to be better storytellers.

Think About...

Ways you can use stories to celebrate the achievements of individuals and teams within your organization.

What key messages can you reinforce by telling effective stories?

Identify sources of inspiration for good stories. These sources may be inside your company or outside of your company. Consider why they inspire you.

Develop a story that you would like to tell a friend about the good things employees in your organization do.

Story = Purpose + Narrative + Honesty

97. | Three Pillars of Inspiration

INSPIRATION IS WHAT PEOPLE look to their leaders to provide. Inspiration is rooted in three attributes:

Realism. Inspirational leaders are rooted in reality. They know the facts but remain undeterred. This sense separates them from fools who are quick to rush into things before considering consequences. Inspirational leaders are keenly aware of what could go wrong and are honest about it. It is this honesty that draws capable contributors. They sense that the leader knows the facts but is willing to experiment as well as persevere.

Improvement. Wanting to make things better is essential to inspiration. Therefore inspirational leaders value innovations. They are inherently creative because they are not satisfied with the status quo. Moreover, they seek to open doors for people who can innovate in their function, be it product development or logistics. They encourage employees to think for themselves.

Optimism. You must believe in the better tomorrow. This is easy to do when the economy is rising but more difficult when it is shrinking. Optimism for the inspirational leader is not merely inherent; it is contagious. Others feel it and want to feed off it. This is essential not only to getting the work done now but also to developing next-generation initiatives that will position the organization for success over the long term.

Inspiration points the way forward
and leaders must deliver.

• • • • • • • •

98. | How to Inspire Others

THERE ARE NO SHORTCUTS when it comes to inspiring others.
Inspiration requires forethought as well as practice.

Inspiration, like motivation, must be organic to the situation. The best way leaders can inspire others is to root the inspiration in the work. To do so they should ask three questions.

What is the significance of what we do? To answer this, leaders must relate the work the team does to the mission and purpose of the organization. It falls to the leader to make the link between individual and team contributions to the accomplishment of the mission. People want to know that their work matters.

How do we measure impact? People are motivated by seeing improvement. The leader must show how the team's contributions enabled the organization to achieve its goals. The leader needs to communicate the success of the organization.

How do we reward outcomes? When the team succeeds, the leader needs to recognize the individual as well as group accomplishments. Recognition and reward for achievement make people feel good about what they have accomplished.

The way in which leaders deliver on the inspiration must be sincere and rooted in the work people do.

Think About...

Ways to derive inspiration from the work you do and the work your team does.

Why is it important to be realistic when addressing inspiration? What happens if you are not grounded in reality?

What is the connection between inspiration and improvement? How can you link the two so people feel more confident in their own abilities?

What specific actions will you take to inspire your people? When will you begin?

Inspiration =
Purpose + Intended Outcome

99. When It's Time to Hang It Up

LEADERS BY NATURE are not quitters. Their strength emerges from their resolve to persevere. Eventually, however, they may need to realize that they are no longer contributing in ways that make the organization stronger.

When that occurs, there are three questions the leader must ask.

Am I able to help the team win? Physical limitations or illness can make the decision easy, but no less painful. Limitations resulting from a failure to perform and a loss of confidence may be more compelling reasons to quit.

Am I hurting the team's ability to succeed? This question gets to the heart of capability. If circumstances prevent a leader from delivering his best, or at least helping others to do their best, stepping aside may be the only recourse.

Can someone else do a better job? Very often a leader with limitations remains the best option, but if there is someone more equipped for the current challenge, the decision to step aside becomes more imperative.

Good leaders must realize when it is time to say
good-bye and in the process allow their team
to achieve something they must deny
themselves—the opportunity to succeed.

Think About...

Knowing when it will be time for you to quit what
you are doing now and move on to something else.

How is your management now enabling people to
succeed?

How is your leadership focusing people on key
challenges that lie ahead?

How do you know you are the right person to lead
your team forward now?

Decision to Step Aside ≅
Organizational Need

100. | Make Time for Yourself Outside of Work

DON'T WAIT TILL YOU RETIRE to develop your outside interests. Here are three suggestions to help you broaden your efforts to create a life beyond work:

Treasure close relationships. For most of us, family is what matters most. Be certain you spend time with those who love you most. There will be years when you are not as available as you may like to be, but never skimp on what you can do when you can do it. And don't forget your friends.

Find a passion outside of work. If you're lucky enough to have a career you love, it can be hard to remember to find a hobby you love, too. But find that hobby and invest in it, whether it's golf, swing dancing, community theater, or whatever else you may enjoy. Just find something that provides another enrichment in your life—and make time for it.

Give of yourself. Find a way to give to your community. Your definition of community is what you want it to be— where you live, where you play, where you worship, or where you seek solace. Yes, your time is limited, but so many of those who live the most fulfilled lives are the busiest! Community is an important part of leading a full life.

Now comes the hard part. All of these things will take

time to develop and nurture, but do take that time. Frankly, research shows that those in their twenties and thirties are much more savvy than my Boomer generation cohorts were about carving out time for what matters most to them.

"The wheel is come full circle," wrote William Shakespeare in *King Lear*—a sobering study of the effect of aging on the powerful. Now is the time to prepare before "the circle" closes too tightly and you have no interests but work itself.

Time + Self = Personal Growth

101. | Six Words to Lead By

A LEADER'S LEGACY BEGINS the day he or she assumes the responsibility to lead others.

A way to think about your legacy and how you shape it is to distill your leadership approach into six words. It is a storytelling technique once practiced by Ernest Hemingway and adopted by many thousands of others.

To help you get started, consider three powerful questions:

What gets me up in the morning? A very basic question! What do you do and why do you do it? For some, the answer is the opportunity to work with others on a project that has real meaning, that is, one that improves the quality of life for others. If this question throws you, consider what you don't like about what you do. Is it possible to change something, or must you change careers?

How can I help others? We humans are motivated to work for goals greater than ourselves. Leaders achieve through the efforts of others. It is imperative that they create conditions in which others can succeed. They help others achieve intentions that enable the team—and by extension the organization—to succeed.

Why do others follow me? Do people follow you because they have to or because they want to? Your influence may stem from your position of authority, but you want others to follow you because they respect your values and trust your example.

Summing up your leadership in six words challenges you to think about the nature of your impact on others and the legacy you will leave in your organization.[17]

"Big idea. Profound thoughts. Truthful moment."

Think About...

Ways you are developing your legacy at work.

Consider ways you make time for yourself outside of the workplace. What do you do that enriches your life? How can you make more time for this source of enrichment?

Give an example of how you would like to be remembered by your colleagues.

Write a six-word memoir that sums up your leadership legacy.

$$\text{Legacy} = \frac{\text{Contribution}}{\text{Time}}$$

Self-Assessment

Consider the following statements and rate your level of agreement with them on a 1–5 scale with 1 being weakest and 5 being strongest.

_____ The team knows that it is my job to set expectations and follow through on them.

_____ The team knows where I stand on the issues.

_____ The team members look to me to explain their roles in fulfilling our mission.

_____ The team believes that I have what it takes to help people do their jobs better.

_____ The team members say that I have their best interests at heart.

_____ The team members believe that my job is to help them succeed as individuals and as a team.

_____ The team members acknowledge my leadership when they bring their problems to me.

_____ The team trusts me to make tough decisions.

_____ The team feels comfortable in raising alternative views in my presence.

_____ The team recognizes that I am one who tries to do what is best for the organization.

_____ **TOTAL SCORE**

+++
50   Perfect (and impossible)
49–30 Keep working
<30   Give yourself credit for being honest

Action Tips for Organizations

Remember that people will value what you do over what you say. Focus on actions more than words.

- Adopt the "what, not how" style of management. Give people an assignment and let them figure out how to do it for themselves. Make yourself available to provide assistance when asked.

- Regard dissent as an opportunity to explore alternatives. Dissent is the best protection against groupthink.

- When you make a hard decision, put the organization first, not yourself.

- Praise your team when it perseveres in the face of adversity. Be available to support team members and be their champion.

- Look on the light side. Life is tough enough without being serious all of the time. Allow for some levity.

- Make a habit of meeting and mingling with all levels of your organization. Listen more than you speak.

- Consider roadblocks as opportunities for learning as well as opportunities for you to lead.

Handbook

THIS SECTION IS A HANDY REFERENCE for management and leadership behaviors that managers need to demonstrate in the workplace in order to build greater levels of trust and achieve intended results.

ORGANIZATIONALLY

Create a shared vision and mission

- Use organizational purpose to develop a clear and concise vision and a well-focused mission statement.
- Communicate the vision clearly and concisely.
- Support the vision with a strong link to the organizational mission.
- Support the vision and mission with organizational values that reinforce positive behaviors.

Develop alignment with mission and strategies

- Communicate the vision widely.
- Invite each team to develop its own vision and mission linked to the organizational mission.
- Develop strategies that reinforce your vision and mission.
- Invite the team to develop tactics to support the strategies.

Build a high-performing organization

- Create teams with individuals whose talents and skills complement one another.

- Instill an innovation ethos that rewards individuals and teams for doing things differently (as long as they are in line with the vision and mission).

- Set goals that challenge the team to stretch and individuals to excel.

- Delegate authority and responsibilities to team leaders. Hold them accountable for results.

- Provide support and resources that teams need to do their work.

- Recognize individuals for exceptional performance.

- Identify individuals worthy of assuming greater levels of authority and responsibility.

INDIVIDUALLY

Be seen

- Visit people where they work.

- Use teleconferences to stay in touch visually with your teams.

- Institute an open-door policy so people can visit you if they need to.

- Hold meetings where the work is done: in the cube, on the shop floor, etc.

Be heard

- Deliver consistent messages. Make your messages clear, coherent, and concise.
- Listen more than you speak.
- Check for understanding.
- Invite feedback from your direct reports (and colleagues, too).

Be there

- Be accessible and available to help always.
- Lead by example, by letting your actions speak louder than your words.
- Act for the good of the team.
- If sacrifice is required, be the first to volunteer.

Coach as you see, hear, and act

- Schedule regular coaching conversations with your direct reports.
- Prepare for them in advance.
- Develop an approach that is based upon constructive conversation where you can counsel, challenge, and encourage your direct reports.
- Learn what makes individuals tick and leverage those motivators.

- Provide constructive criticism that affirms individual contributions as well as provides insight into further development.

- Insist that every employee have a development plan that covers work goals and professional goals.

Acknowledgments

THE THINKING REFLECTED IN THIS BOOK is the result of the many good men and women whom I have had the opportunity to teach and coach. It was their questions as well as their insights that led me to develop this book.

Some portions of this book have been adapted from my work for publications including HBR.org, FastCompany.com, Inc.com, and WashingtonPost.com/On Leadership. I also want to give a special thank-you to Sarah Green at Harvard Business Review and Lillian Cunningham of WashingtonPost.com/On Leadership for encouraging my contributions.

I am indebted to Mark Royal, a principal in the Chicago office of the Hay Group. Mark and his team provided me with the data contained in the research sections of this book. Also, thanks to Andrea Friedman of Bliss Public Relations for making the introduction.

My friend Kathy Macdonald deserves mention for helping me think through the process of creating this book.

I owe special thanks to Christina Parisi, my editor at AMACOM Books, who was receptive to the idea of this book and has encouraged me all the way. I also want to thank my copyeditor, Kate Petrella, for her help. Thanks also go to my agent, Jeff Herman.

And as with all of my books, I thank Gail Campanella, my wife and love, for her insights and support.

Notes

SELF

1. Adapted from "How to Crack the Self-Awareness Paradigm," HBR.org, December 23, 2009.

2. Note adaptation of quote by James MacGregor Burns from his book *Leadership* (New York: Harper Perennial/Torchbook, 1979), pp. 9–45 (paperback edition).

3. Adapted from "Leadership Is More than a Buzz Word," WashingtonPost.com/On Leadership, October 4, 2010.

4. Adapted from "Flunking the Accountability Test," WashingtonPost.com/On Leadership, March 30, 2010.

5. Adapted from "To Lead More Effectively, Boost Your Confidence," HBR.org, July 13, 2009.

6. Adapted from "Finding Hope in Troubled Times," HBR.org, December 3, 2009; Paul Johnson *Churchill* (New York: Viking, 2009).

7. Adapted from "The Value of Being an Underdog," CBSi/BNET, May 23, 2011.

8. John Wooden quote: http://www.hoopsu.com/99-wisdoms-from-wooden.

9. Adapted from "Managing Your Own Fears," HBR.org, October 8, 2008.

10. Adapted from "What a 100 Year Old Coach Can Teach Us About Leadership," FastCompany.com, September 7, 2010. This piece is inspired by advice given to Lloyd Carr, former head coach of the University of Michigan, by Red Simmons, himself a former collegiate and Olympic track coach.

COLLEAGUES

1. Adapted from "Secret to Leadership? Keeping It Simple" from CBS MoneyWatch, December 12, 2011. The author would like to acknowledge two works that contributed to this section: Michael Useem, *The Leader's Checklist: 15 Mission-Critical Principles* (Philadelphia, PA: Wharton Digital Press, 2011) and Jim Collins and Morten Hansen, *Great by Choice* (New York: Harper Business, 2011).

2. Adapted from "Combating the 'Not My Job' Mentality," CBSi/BNET, April 19, 2011.

3. Adapted from "5 Ways to Influence People Who Do Not Report to You," Fastcompany.com, December 9, 2010.

4. Adapted from "Leading Your Peers: How to Do It Right" CBSi/BNET, September 6, 2011. This piece was inspired by Dave Davies, "Covering the Plate: A Baseball Catcher Tells All," NPR Fresh Air, August 18, 2011: http://www.npr.org/2011/08/18/139649031/covering-the-plate-a-baseball-catcher-tells-all.

5. Adapted from "Avoid Burnout by Focusing on Your Team," HBR.org, November 8, 2010.

6. Adapted from "How Successful Leaders Improve Their Team's Performance," CBSi/BNET, October 24, 2011.

7. Adapted from "Are You a Supportive Teammate?" CBSi/BNET, May 15, 2011.

8. Adapted from "Is Your Staff Too Nice?" CBSi/BNET, April 21, 2011.

9. Adapted from "Is Your Staff Too Nice?" CBSi/BNET, April 21, 2011.

10. Adapted from "Tips for Making Small Talk with Bigwigs," HBR.org, March 22, 2010.

11. Adapted from "Lead Through Your Boss," WashingtonPost.com/On Leadership, April 22, 2010.

12. Adapted from "How to Recognize (and Cure) Your Own Hubris," HBR.org, posted by John Baldoni on September 8, 2010.

13. Adapted from "How to Recognize (and Cure) Your Own Hubris," HBR.org, posted by John Baldoni on September 8, 2010.

14. Adapted from "Cubicle Coaching," FastCompany.com, April 11, 2007; the author would also like to acknowledge the work of executive coach Jodi Knox, Ph.D., who was interviewed for the original article.

ORGANIZATION

1. Paul Hersey, behavioral scientist and businessman, is widely credited as the theorist behind "situational leadership," a process of managing and leading in response to changing circumstances. http://en.wikipedia.org/wiki/Paul_Hersey.

2. Adapted from "Know When to Manage Behind the Scenes," CBSi/BNET, August 5, 2011.

3. This was inspired by the example of Jim Shepard, former CEO of Canfor, who was cited in Gordon Pitts, Iain Marlow, and Greg Keenan, "Ditch the Yes Men," *Globe and Mail*, June 23, 2011.

4. Adapted from "Take Conflict Out of Management," Inc.com, December 1, 2011.

5. Adapted from "Go Against the Grain," WashingtonPost.com/On Leadership, October 12, 2010.

6. Joe Nocera, "Running G.E., Comfortable in His Skin," *New York Times*, June 9, 2007.

7. Adapted from "Judging Talent by What You See, Hear and Understand," FastCompany.com, August 8, 2010, citing methods developed by Rich Cho, general manager of the Portland Trailblazers when this article was published.

8. Adapted from "Strong Character Trumps Perfection," WashingtonPost.com/On Leadership, December 13, 2010.

9. Adapted from "The Toyota Edition: Why CEOs Fail," WashingtonPost.com/On Leadership, February 11, 2010.

10. Adapted from "The Audacity to Delegate," WashingtonPost.com/On Leadership, November 12, 2009.

11. Adapted from "Don't Let the Bear Market Ruin Morale," CBSi/BNET, August 11, 2011.

12. Adapted from "Leaders Need to Involve Themselves in Crises," WashingtonPost.com/On Leadership, August 24, 2010.

13. Adapted from "Don't Wing Your Next Crisis," FastCompany.com, September 14, 2010.

14. Adapted from "Is There a Common Cause?" WashingtonPost.com/On Leadership, July 19, 2010.

15. Author's coaching questions adapted from Ellis Avery, "Digging Up the Depths of Desire," *Wall Street Journal*, February 25, 2012.

16. Adapted from "Four Ways to Evaluate Such a Big Decision," WashingtonPost.com/On Leadership, November 22, 2010.

17. Adapted from "Sum Up Your Leadership in Six Words," HBR.org, June 9, 2009. Also citing Neal Conan, "Life Stories Distilled in Six Words," NPR Books, February 7, 2008, http://www.npr.org/templates/story/story.php?storyId=18768430. For more information on six-word memoirs, read Rachel Ferschleiser and Larry Smith (editors), *Not Quite What I Was Planning: Six Word Memoirs by Writers Famous and Obscure* (New York: Harper Perennial, 2008).

About the Author

JOHN BALDONI is the president of Baldoni Consulting LLC, a full-service executive coaching and leadership development firm. He is an internationally recognized leadership educator and executive coach and the author of many books, including *Lead with Purpose, Lead Your Boss*, and *Great Motivation Secrets of Great Leaders*. John speaks throughout North America and Europe, and in 2012 Leadership Gurus International ranked him No. 10 on its list of global leadership experts. John has authored more than 400 leadership columns for a variety of online publications including *CBS MoneyWatch, Harvard Business Review*, and *Inc.* His leadership resource website is www.johnbaldoni.com.